HOW CAN WE KEEP CHRISTIAN MARRIAGES FROM FALLING APART?

HOW CAN WE KEEP CHRISTIAN MARRIAGES FROM FALLING APART?

Gerald L. Dahl

publishers since 1798

THOMAS NELSON PUBLISHERS
Nashville

To the couples whose commitment to their marriages through the counseling process gives hope to others

Published in Nashville, Tennessee, by Thomas Nelson, Inc. and distributed in Canada by Lawson Falle, Ltd., Cambridge, Ontario.

Printed in the United States of America.

Library of Congress Cataloging-in-Publication Data

Dahl, Gerald L.
How can we keep christian marriages from falling apart / Gerald L. Dahl.
p. cm.
Bibliography: p.
ISBN 0-8407-3117-5 : 6.95
1. Marriage—Religious aspects—Christianity. I. Title.
BV835.D32 1988
248.8'4—dc19 88-36827
CIP

ISBN 0-8407-3117-5

Contents

Preface vii
1. Once Was Not Enough 9
2. The Invisible Pain on the Other Side 17
3. Remember? You Promised 22
4. God Designed You Not to Be Alone 39
5. Too Good to Be Real 50
6. Twice They Were Strangers 61
7. What to Do When the Feelings Are Gone 71
8. Communication: The Food That Feeds Your Marriage 87
9. From Saturday Night Mistress to Sunday Morning Saint 100
10. The Double Bind 107
11. Every Married Person Needs an Affair 116
12. Confession/Forgiveness: The Only Road to Restoration 124
13. The Power of Submission 143
14. Fun Is Serious Business 152
15. Security for Your Marriage 159
16. The Plus Element 168
17. Will It Ever Be Like It Was? 175
Study Guide 177
Notes 190

Preface

As our society shoots the rapids of social change, every institution and social value is called into question. Marriage is no exception. Although it continues to be the core unit of our society, marriage is now taking a battering from soaring divorce rates. For years Christians have smugly watched the climbing rates; however, this tragic epidemic of marital failure has now reached into the church.

Ten years ago I wrote a book called *Why Christian Marriages Are Breaking Up* to alert Christians that divorce was infiltrating the church at an alarming rate. Although the Word of God defines marriage as a permanent bond, persons claiming faith in Christ have been terminating the holy union, and divorce has become a common occurrence in the church. My book called for Christian couples to seek solutions to their marriage problems by staying *in* the marriage rather than by abandoning their vows. From my experience in the marriage counseling office, I have discovered that what hurting spouses are seeking can best be found in their marriage instead of in divorce.

In August 1987 *Newsweek* reported that for the first time in decades the divorce rate was dropping. Throughout the nation the growing number of couples reconsidering their marriage before seeking a divorce has confirmed the message of my book. This trend must continue, and the church, the body of believers that live by faith in Jesus Christ, should set the standard.

This revision of the original book is offered to that end. You will find the chapters that show how to maintain a strong marriage remain unchanged. Other chapters have been expanded, and new ones have been added to deal with the stresses facing marriages today.

Violated marital vows have prompted many couples to believe their marriage is over and to impulsively turn to divorce. This need not happen. As serious as a situation may be, restoration is nearly always possible and best for almost everyone.

At times as I have written this book, I have revisited certain life experiences and found them warm and refreshing. At other times the confrontation has been painful. As you read, I know that your experience will be the same. This subject touches us at the most intimate point in our lives.

I am grateful to the people, too numerous to name, who have continued to be a part of my life and who have contributed to the writing of this book. May our struggles and victories give hope to all who seek God's direction in their lives.

Gerald L. Dahl

Chapter One

Once Was Not Enough

A familiar quietness fell over the reception area as the answering service took over the telephone calls and the last patients of the day left their therapy sessions. The waiting room that had been filled with the emotion and drama of troubled lives was now empty. Office doors were locked and the voices of staff personnel faded in the hallways as they went their separate ways.

The clinic was almost deserted on this late Thursday afternoon except for a few of us who led evening therapy groups. I was one of them. For years in my marriage counseling practice I had devoted this particular evening to group therapy for couples. It had become so routine that everyone in my family knew Thursday night and "Daddy's late night" were synonymous. These evenings were often exhausting, as couples would expose in vivid detail the crises that threatened to destroy their marriage relationships. Long ago I had learned that relationships, like individuals, can become critically ill. Certainly the termination of a relationship has some of the same profound effects upon people as does the actual loss of someone through physical death.

I never knew exactly what to expect as my five couples would come together each week for their one-and-a-half-hour session. Sometimes the atmosphere was warm and caring; other times it was hostile and tense, often requiring an extension of the session to give the couples some means to continue together until they returned the next Thursday.

Although the sessions varied from week to week, this one was to be unique. Tonight was to be a first for the clinic, and it was to happen in *our* group. Knowing there are few things left to distinguish themselves as "firsts," I had asked several of my colleagues what they felt was "the least likely thing you would expect to happen in couples' group therapy." I received many very interesting responses, but not one of them had been able to guess correctly. What's more, they had not even believed the answer when I told them!

Tonight there was to be a *wedding* in our couples' session—an honest-to-goodness, genuine, bonafide wedding! There would be a license, a minister, a ceremony, and everything else to make the event legal and official. As for me, I was more nervous and excited than if I were the father of the bride.

I realized that my joy and excitement was for more than just the wedding. What could be more thrilling for a marriage counselor than to share in the experience of bringing a couple *back* together to say their vows a second time! We were resurrecting a marriage that had been declared legally dead.

The bride and groom were Donna and Mark, a Christian couple who had been married for twenty-one years. They had raised two children and had what appeared to be a successful marriage. No one had known they had problems, including Mark. But two years ago Donna had announced to him that she was tired of the prison she found herself in and was going to divorce him.

"My needs aren't being met, and I have to find out who I really am," she told him as she presented the divorce papers. At that time she did not consider marriage counseling an option. She moved out, leaving Mark stunned and single.

It took her only a short time to realize she had made a terrible mistake. What she had been looking for was latent—but present—right in her previous marriage relationship.

She came to Mark, telling him how God had touched her life. Her eyes had been opened to see the priceless treasure she had abandoned by breaking the covenant they had made. She asked his forgiveness, hoping that somewhere in his heart he would have a desire to try again. Donna told Mark she realized her needs could never be met in the same way outside the marriage as they could be with him. She carried a mixture of peace and apprehension within her. She knew now that Jesus Christ was again in control of *her* life, but she was apprehensive as to whether or not Mark could trust her enough to let her back into *his* life.

Mark was still in love; he had never stopped loving Donna. But still numb from the shock of rejection and divorce, he was scared to try again. He wanted to shake off his feelings, but they stuck with him like a magnet. Have you ever desperately wanted something but were too frightened to reach out and take the chance of getting hurt again? This is where Mark was when Donna came back to him and said, "I love you and want to live with you for the rest of my life."

Shortly thereafter they came to my office, nervously introduced themselves, and told me their story. They sensed the need for professional help before going any further in repairing their relationship. Mark said, "I have never experienced a pain as severe as when Donna told me she was leaving. I couldn't handle it if it were to happen again." Although understandably frightened, he asked me to help him overcome his fears so he could once again trust his wife. I assured him that his very presence in my office was a beginning of this trust.

Although I said nothing about this at the time, I determined to check out very closely his wife's sincerity in her renewed commitment to him. Nothing is more destructive to a person than repeated rejection. Eventually that person finds it nearly impossible to trust *anyone,* even though the desire and basis for trust may be there.

We accepted them into our group, and they began to attend our sessions. Remarriage was brought up to them from time to time by the other group members, but during those first few sessions it was quickly dropped or sidestepped in favor of a more comfortable subject. Even though they were both interested in remarriage, their insecurity was reflected by the eggshells they walked on whenever the subject came up.

One day nearly six months into our weekly sessions, I received a telephone call from Donna. "Great news!" she said, "Mark and I have talked, and we are ready to get married again." Before I could express my elation over their decision, she continued. "There's more. We want to be married in the Thursday group. We feel closer to these people than anyone else in the world, and we want to share our joy with them."

I listened as Donna emphasized that they wanted it to be a simple ceremony at the end of the regular session with only our group members in attendance. They were sensitive to the fact that people in the group would still have matters they needed to discuss in therapy. Mark and Donna wanted them to be sure to have plenty of time for sharing personal needs before the wedding. We set the date.

Tonight was the wedding. Everyone arrived at the usual time to take their places in the circle, carrying on light conversation that often preceded the session. After a few minutes I walked in, closed the door, loosened my tie, and rolled up my shirt sleeves. These gestures have become a silent signal that the group session is beginning, so the conversation quieted.

My eyes scanned the circle. Everyone looked the same except for Donna, who was sitting beautifully poised in her long dress, and Mark in a new suit and fresh haircut. They sat quietly, politely indicating that they preferred just to listen during the first part of our session, knowing their time was to come later.

During the opening moments of the session, I usually collect my thoughts and study facial expressions and other nonverbal messages of group members as a key to know where to begin. Tonight it was different; they were watching me for the same reason. I expressed my joy and satisfaction over what was going to happen later in the evening and explained that we would have group as usual for about an hour. Then we would stop to have the wedding.

With that our session began. Tom talked about the stress he was experiencing in his job and the effect it was having on his marriage. Jan and Larry shared about their rough week and expressed uncertainty regarding the future of their relationship. Mark, who was usually reluctant to talk, responded with authority, telling them dissolving their marriage would give them far more serious problems than they were facing now. Donna jumped in with a dose of warm support and sincere faith that Jan and Larry would find the happiness she and Mark now had. It occurred to me that when they left the group I would miss the tremendous encouragement she gave to others.

At nine I heard the front door of the reception area open. Doug, an ordained minister in private practice as a marriage counselor, walked down the hallway. We had been friends for years, so I was especially pleased when he consented to conduct the ceremony. His long black clergy robe added dignity to the occasion.

We rearranged the chairs into rows and moved furniture, leaving an open area at one end of the room for the wedding party. Meanwhile, Mark and Donna were getting acquainted with Doug in my office across the hall. I caught myself dashing back and forth between the group room and my office, telling myself, *This cannot be happening—not in group therapy on Thursday night at the clinic!*

As Donna, Mark, and Doug entered, a hush came over the room. Doug looked at me and said, "Jerry, they want you to be best man."

I jumped to my feet with the same enthusiasm I had had in high school when the football coach called me off the bench to enter the game. Doug reminded the couple that they needed one more witness for the ceremony. Donna extended her hand to Karen, who was usually very shy. However, today she confidently stood to her feet and joined the rest of the wedding party.

The room now possessed the sacredness of a chapel, and I knew the presence of the Lord was there. Doug prayed, inviting God's blessing upon what was about to take place.

I was extremely proud of Doug. I realized that my relationship with him was usually as a colleague in marriage counseling. But tonight he was more. He was a minister of the gospel, God's servant with divine authority to conduct this sacred rite.

Doug's presence reminded me that marriage is far more than a mere legal event. It is a holy agreement designed by God to exist above all other human relationships. I often emphasized to my students at Bethel College that marriage is divinely designed and uniquely sacred.

The silence was broken as we heard those familiar words:

> Dearly beloved, we are gathered together here in the sight of God and in the presence of this company, to join together this man and this woman in holy matrimony.
>
> Marriage is an honorable estate, instituted of God, blessed by our Lord Jesus Christ, and commended by St. Paul to be honorable among all men.[1]

As I listened to the words, they came at me with special meaning. What was happening in this little group therapy room *was* "in the sight of God . . . and in the presence of this company."

What a company! I thought. Donna and Mark had only known these people for a short time, yet they were closer to them than lifelong friends. These couples identified, shared, and talked openly with each other about the problems of their relationships. I was pleased with all of them for trying to heal their marriages instead of walking away from them. As I glanced over my shoulder I saw several couples holding hands, and I hoped they, too, were renewing their vows in their hearts.

Doug reminded Mark and Donna that this covenant was not to be entered into lightly or unadvisedly, but reverently, soberly, and in the fear of God. They did not need much reminding. Tonight they were saying with total commitment the vows they had exchanged in their teens, twenty-three years earlier.

As Doug asked Mark to repeat that section of the vows

requiring the "I will," Donna's eyes, filled with love, never left Mark's face. Eagerly taking her turn, she recited her vows, which seemed indelibly written in her mind. Then came the key moment. "Do you solemnly promise, before God and these witnesses, that forsaking all others for him alone, you will perform unto him all the duties that a wife owes to her husband, until God, by death, shall separate you?"

There was a moment of silence, not reflecting any hesitancy but instead giving the moment the solemnity it deserved. I watched as Donna's eyes, having already said *yes,* took on a special glisten and she replied with a confident, loving, "I will."

A broad smile came over Mark's face. His fear and the insecurity of losing his wife were gone for good. For this couple who had become so special to all of us, *once was not enough.* They had, by God's grace, received a second chance.

The solemn mood of the ceremony quickly lightened as the group moved into the clinic waiting room. It had become the banquet hall for the reception. The table usually filled with tattered magazines, worn from being nervously paged by waiting patients, now hosted a beautiful buffet of food that the newlyweds had insisted on providing. Our clinic had added its part to the evening by providing a three-tiered wedding cake.

Throughout the evening, the excitement never diminished. As the couples began to leave I could sense they were still trying to grasp the fact that they had been to both a group therapy session and a wedding.

Finding myself alone, I walked back into the group room and drained the last cup of coffee from the pot. Sitting with my feet up and the lights out, I watched the couples go to their cars in the parking lot below. Donna and Mark were last, their arms filled with plates, cups, and the remains of the buffet. The wedding was over and a new marriage had begun. As they drove off, I sensed a satisfaction reserved only for marriage counselors after watching a happy ending.

But all kinds of questions began tumbling through my

head. Why are so many Christian marriages falling by the wayside? Why are the marriages of evangelical leaders, pastors, and other spiritual pacesetters breaking up? Why did Mark and Donna's marriage fail the first time? What made Donna want to try again? What happens when Christian marriages fail, and for what reasons are some saved?

My eyes turned back again to the parking lot. I thought about the other couples. How many would see no future in staying together and ultimately get a divorce?

Chapter Two

The Invisible Pain on the Other Side

"Divorce is emotionally like a massive heart attack that leaves you disabled and in pain."

This was the vivid description Mary gave me as she recounted her own recent divorce. Mary is a nurse at a medical center and is a strong, confident person who is well experienced in her profession. But her divorce struck her down in a way she had never previously experienced, even though she had known other crises in her life.

Despite the fact that both she and her husband felt that divorce was their best choice, it was extremely painful for her. She missed several months of work and was hospitalized for depression as a result of the trauma.

At one point it was nearly fatal. With a shaky voice she told me how she had sat alone for hours in the middle of the night, staring at the pills that could end her life. Because of her medical background she knew the exact number for a lethal overdose.

There they were, counted out on the kitchen table, awaiting her decision. Through God's protective love she chose to go on living. But when she looked back on the whole experience she told me, "Never again do I want to experience *that pain*. It was terrible and nothing seemed to make it go away."

Eventually, Mary started to recover, and today she is doing quite well as a single person. But the painful effects of the divorce will always remain with her. More than a year later, as she was shopping alone one night at a local mall, she suddenly found herself face to face with her ex-husband. Their eyes met and they both froze. Neither knew just what to do. After a long moment, they passed without speaking.

Mary's wound was opened once again. She ran out of the shopping center with tears streaming down her face. She was so upset that it took her more than an hour to find her car in the parking lot. A week off work and a couple of counseling sessions helped start the healing once again.

"The pain will always be there," she said, "but now I think I have it in a place where it will not interfere as easily with my day-to-day living."

I asked Mary if she knew why the pain was so intense, especially since the divorce had been her choice as well as her husband's. Her answer included many factors relating to the profound readjustment she was required to make. There was less money and more work. She was now responsible for little things she had previously taken for granted, such as having the car serviced and buying snow tires for winter.

However, one reason seemed to stand out above all the others. When you get a divorce you choose to end your marriage relationship. However, with that choice you also terminate other relationships that you want and need. In one way or another a divorce affects almost all your relationships, shaking the very foundation of your support system.

In Mary's situation, by divorcing her husband she also lost a set of parents-in-law she had grown to love. Mary had never known her natural father because he died when she was an infant. Therefore, her husband's father had been especially close to her.

Through the marriage Mary had also developed a relationship with a sister-in-law who had become her best friend. They vowed to continue the friendship in spite of the divorce, but after three months they never saw each other again.

All the couples with whom Mary and her husband had socialized assured her she was still part of the gang. But after a couple of parties where she was the only single person there, the invitations and contacts stopped.

Mary's story is just one of many. The painful experience is the same; only the people are different. Please hear me when I tell you that a large part of the pain of divorce comes from the fact that with the *voluntary termination* of the marriage, many other relationships are *terminated involuntarily*. Your old support system is gone. A new one must be built. But in the interim, you are alone.

DIVORCE: AN EXCHANGE NOT A SOLUTION

Divorce is not a solution, but rather an exchange of problems. You give up one set of frustrations only to take on another. You may walk away from your marital problems, but you take on others that are just as bad, if not worse. No matter who you are or what the circumstances of your marriage, you will experience in divorce a whole new set of emotional and social upheavals that you never dreamed were possible.

Listen to the plea of a missionary's former wife as we discussed counsel she would give to Christians with marriage difficulties: "If they are considering divorce as an option, I'd like to shout, scream, stomp, and yell that it's not the best way out. Even if they see it as a moral option, the grass on the other side is not necessarily greener, and sometimes only brown and dry."

The overwhelming majority of couples choose divorce far too quickly as a solution to their marriage problems, only to awaken in disillusionment over their new single status. In the Twin Cities area, social workers in divorce courts prepare people for the reality of divorce by acquainting them with the five phases of loss experienced in death as outlined by Elisabeth Kübler-Ross: *denial, depression, anger, bargaining,* and *a form of acceptance*.[1] I believe it is an accurate comparison to equate divorce with death as far as the emotional experience is concerned.

Divorce is not a solution. Only now, after years of exposure to the pain of those going through divorce, do I begin to understand God's powerful response, "For I *hate* divorce, says the Lord the God of Israel [italics mine]."[2]

Even we who know Christ and seek to follow Him have been bought off by a comfort-loving society in which many people see marriage as a temporary state to be honored "as long as we both shall love." After all, what do we do in our culture when we become impatient with something that is inconvenient? We get rid of it. The liberalization of abortion laws is a prime example of this mentality. Or we may trade in an inconvenient thing for a different one. Living in an era of disposables, exchange and replacement have become so automatic in solving our problems that we apply it to marriage without a second thought.

Actually, isn't remarriage often an exchange or replacement of spouses? I believe this is *always* the case when someone divorces for the purpose of marrying another. We change jobs, homes, cars, churches, and anything else that may become inconvenient or interfere with our comfort and independence. It only follows that one out of three couples "solve" their marriage problems by divorce. They also find new problems equal to or worse than the original ones.

TAKE A CLOSER LOOK

If you are considering divorce, let me advise you to take a close look at what you are doing *before* you start any action. Let me repeat: Most couples begin to dissolve their marriages before they realize what is happening.

One business executive I was seeing was having difficulty deciding whether or not to divorce his wife. Although his Christian commitment was not clear to me, he definitely was the conscientious, habitual churchgoing type. Since he was also a pragmatic man, I suggested he set up a divorce balance sheet, listing on one side the gains of the divorce and on the other side the losses—including financial.

At our next session he told me without hesitation that he had determined to remain married. From that exercise he realized the problems he had did not compare with those he would take on in a divorce. His pragmatic reasoning was unromantic, but it got him off dead center and pointed to the exchange of problems that occurs in a divorce. (Incidentally, with a significant amount of effort from each individual, this couple is again finding romance as well.)

I am aware that there are exceptional cases, where physical abuse and threats to life determine the future of a marriage. In one church the elders actually had to order a divorce through the courts because of the brutality of a husband who battered his wife over the span of several months. In this case they did well. But let's face the facts: We have made the exception the rule. Divorce in the evangelical church has become O.K. Not much is said against it any longer. Society has tainted us.

While we continue in our legalism in so many areas where Scripture does *not* speak out, we have become licentious in the matter of divorce—where it *does* speak out. I realize that saving a failing marriage can be a trying experience, but in the end it is worth it. It is time to turn things around and regain righteousness.

For the Christian, divorce is not an option. You promised God and each other that you would stay married for life. Let's look at how it can be done.

Chapter Three

Remember? You Promised

June 24, 1960. It was a hot summer evening. The ushers were trying to adjust the church doors to allow more air circulation throughout the sanctuary without causing the candles at the front to melt too quickly.

Earlier in the day I had helped my father install lightning rods on the top of a barn roof. He owned a rural hardware business and desperately needed my help with that job. Besides, I needed some distraction until evening. (I also used the time to practice my wedding vows, for we had decided to memorize them for our ceremony. By the time I had worked halfway across the barn roof, I had my vows down cold.)

The day passed quickly. Now I found myself waiting in a little side room at the front of the church with my brother Glenn, our best man. A door to the outside was propped open, exposing a lazy sun, setting behind a large grove of oak trees. I had successfully *acted* calm and somewhat relaxed all day, especially around my brother. But now my heart skipped a beat and I swallowed hard as the organ began sending forth the strains of Bach's "Jesu, Joy of Man's Desiring." I knew my time had finally come.

Just as Glenn started into the sanctuary he pointed to the open door and said with a mischievous grin, "There's your last chance if you want to take it." With that, he disappeared into the church. He had a knack for coming up with choice statements at the most opportune (or inopportune) moments.

Alone and waiting to enter, I looked again through the open door to the outside. The sun had disappeared behind the trees. Suddenly I realized how alone I felt. *Yet,* I thought, *in a few moments I will be with Judy, and I will no longer be alone.*

Lord, I am ready to make my promise, I said in my heart, and I passed through the door into the sanctuary, finding myself in front of what seemed like a million people. All I could see were faces and eyes, legions of them, all looking at me.

Even with Glenn beside me I felt alone and very much on display. My eyes moved about the sanctuary, not knowing where to look. One by one the attendants entered.

Then Judy started down the aisle. With our eyes fixed upon each other, I became completely unaware of everything else. She had never looked more beautiful. In her flowing white dress, her face hiding behind the bridal veil, she moved gracefully toward me. Right then I wanted to shout and leap for joy. I thought, *Lord, thank You for this beautiful bride You are giving me to be my wife.*

The intensity heightened as I reached out and we touched. Judy gently took my arm and together we climbed the stairs of the platform to face the minister. The majestic organ was now silent, and in the hush of the moment the minister said, "Let us pray."

REDISCOVER PAST FEELINGS

I could easily continue recalling for you detail after detail of that special evening in our lives. But now I want you to shift your thoughts and images from our wedding to your own. Recall in vivid detail the golden moments of that day when *you promised* before God and witnesses to love, honor, and cherish your partner in holy wedlock. Let your mind float freely, allowing yourself to remember the events of your wedding that have been tucked away in your memory for years. If you can effectively lose yourself in the history of that day, you will find that you not only recall the facts, but you can also reexperience the feelings.

The recall potential God has given us is great. The human

brain is like a complex computer that has permanently recorded not only facts but also feelings. Therefore, it is possible not only to *remember* but also to *relive* the spontaneous, involuntary feelings of events from our past.

Dr. Wilder Penfield, a neurosurgeon who has done significant research in this area, reports, "Perhaps the most significant discovery was that not only past events are recorded in detail but also the feelings that were associated with those events. An event and the feeling which was produced by the event are inextricably locked together in the brain so that one cannot be evoked without the other."[1]

Apply this principle to yourself and seek out both the facts and feelings of your past. Try to recall those early experiences with your spouse as you grew to know and love each other. If you can really get into it, you will once again find some of the old feelings that accompanied those events. Physically returning to the setting where it happened is sure to help. It always happens to us when we visit the church where we met.

Find that compartment in your mind, and relive your wedding day. Can you rediscover the setting and the feelings you had for each other? Do you remember the promises you made? How did you feel as you held your partner's hand and said your vows?

RECALL PAST PROMISES

Let me help you recall the promises you made and the meaning behind them:

> Dearly beloved, we are gathered together here in the sight of God, and in the presence of these witnesses, to join together this man and this woman in holy matrimony.[2]

PUBLIC COMMITMENT: DON'T GO IT ALONE

If you have not had the experience of serving in public office, in the military, or as a witness in court, your wedding was most likely the only time in your life when you solemnly and *officially* gave a personal promise. At the onset you were reminded that this moment was not only a human, social, legal event but also a sacred one—"in the sight of God." God was present and was very much a part of your special moment. His presence continues throughout your marriage.

Your public vows also recognized another significant presence—"these witnesses." Think back to those who attended your wedding. Whether the group was small or large, your guests, by their presence, made a statement of their investment in the success of your marital commitment.

I saw clearly the significance of public vows when I was interviewed for a television talk show. Before the show, Sandy, the hostess, confided that she had been married for only seven weeks.

Although she was in her midthirties, this was her first marriage. She had lived with a former boyfriend for more than two years, but that relationship had come to an abrupt, unhappy ending.

Following the telecast we went to get a cup of coffee.

"I'm really pleased we have this chance to talk," she said.

"You're just the kind the person I've been wanting to talk with as well," I replied.

"Why is that?"

"Frequently, couples ask me why they need to be married. They ask if a marriage license really makes a difference, telling me that 'A commitment had better be more than a piece of paper.'

"I try to explain that it certainly is but that a marriage ceremony and all it involves is necessary to fully experience this commitment. They accuse me of having a biased attitude, since I've been happily married to the same woman for twenty years.

"Here is where I need your help, Sandy. From your viewpoint, is there really a difference between being married and just living together?"

"All the difference in the world!" she immediately responded.

I settled back and listened as she told her story. She and her former boyfriend had never really planned to live together. It had just happened. One night he slept over and soon after that the event became a habit that neither of them ever talked about. But Sandy always had a nagging fear that someday her lover would leave her.

Two years later her fear became a reality. One night she returned to an empty apartment and a "good-bye" note on the kitchen table. The hurt of his departure was like the searing pain of a divorce, but she could not elicit understanding and sympathy from her friends. After all, they had just been living together. Sandy said it took a long time for her to regain her trust in men.

"Now that you're married," I asked, "do you ever experience that same fear with your husband?"

"I sure do," she replied, pausing, "but it only lasts for a brief moment."

"Why?" I asked curiously.

"Whenever that fear invades my mind, I recall our wedding and relive our ceremony and the vows. Not only was God present and listening, but also the minister and more than one hundred of our friends and relatives were there. They all heard us make our promises. That helps give me security!" she concluded.

Marriage is usually an event in which many people, including family, friends, and the church, have invested. Witnesses need to be there to support you, not only on that special day but also throughout the years of your marriage. It is a group commitment. Don't go it alone. This is all part of your ceremony and vows.

FOUR KEYS TO MARRIAGE

In another integral part of the ceremony, you promised to ". . . love, comfort, honor and keep [him/her], in sickness and in health; and, forsaking all others, keep only unto [him/her], so long as you both shall live."[3] Love, comfort, honor, and keep are unique promises that play a key role in marriage. Let's look at each one.

Love

Most of us have all experienced "I love you" messages from family and friends before the time of our marriage. But do you really understand the meaning of those three words, *I love you?*

In my marriage and family class at Bethel College, I would often ask for a show of hands of students who had said that they loved someone romantically. Slowly the hands of students would rise as they exposed this intimate part of themselves. Next, I would ask the meaning of those words. Now the struggle would begin as they attempted the difficult task of defining *love* using other words. (Try it yourself!)

"My most special friend," one student once offered.

"I would do anything to please," stated another.

"Willing to give totally of myself for the other person's happiness," said a third.

Writing these comments on the chalkboard, I affirmed them as excellent examples of altruistic devotion, often regarded by the church as agape love, reflective of God's love for us. We agreed to the validity of these definitions, but we recognized that they were not uniquely applicable to our romantic partner.

Blushes appeared as I pressed them to recall the first time "I love you" had entered their romantic life. Why the red faces? What makes romantic love unique, provoking such a response from these lovers? After an uncomfortable silence in the classroom as students struggled to find the appropriate response, the predictable answer emerged in a whisper, "Sex."

"Correct!" I replied.

Romantic love is certainly more than sex, but it is the *sexual element* that offers a wonderful uniqueness to this God-given love. Essentially, romance is a hybrid form of love in which the altruism of agape love blends with sexual attraction to create a bonding intended only for marriage. *This is the context in which the sexual element is to be introduced and nurtured to the culmination of the marriage bed.* As we read in Hebrews

13:4: "Marriage is honorable among all, and the bed undefiled."

During your wedding ceremony, when you promised "to love," you offered a unique love to your partner, intended only for the two of you to share.

Comfort

Comfort means to care about a person in a gentle, supportive way. There will be times when your spouse needs comfort and you do not feel like giving it. Remember, in your vows you promised to comfort. So give comfort, when it's needed, in a way you know your partner will appreciate. This means being sensitive and supportive when your spouse is hurting.

Honor

Honor means you promise to hold each other in highest esteem. This helps protect you from destructive power struggles that divide many marriages.

Bill and Polly, a married couple in my class, perpetually argued over who should submit to whom. The only difference in their situation from the usual debate was that their positions were reversed. Polly believed Bill was the head of their marriage. Whatever he said was the final word, and she was to submit. Bill, however, claimed they were equal with differing roles. In Bill's mind, his authority was not an issue.

"You are head of this marriage. Tell me what to do," Polly would plead.

"No! We are equals," Bill would firmly reply. And so the debate continued.

One day it appeared that the arguing had finally ceased. So I asked if it had.

"Yes, we have resolved it," said Bill.

"How?" I asked.

"I told Polly that I was the head of this marriage and that everything I said was final."

"That's right, Bill," was her quick response.

" 'Then,' I said, 'carefully listen to me because I am only

going to say this once,'" continued Bill. "'I decree that we are equal, and I never want you to bring it up again.'"

I chuckled with them at the humorous side of this exchange. They were newlyweds, deeply in love, experiencing the results of a couple's attempt to "honor" each other. We may question their theological position, but when honor is present, destructive competition ceases.

Keep

How does the little word *keep* fit into the vows? *Keep* implies a special form of possessing. The word means that you will continue to belong to each other in a permanent union, no matter what.

During the early years of my childhood, we boys would try to be men in every aspect as we walked along Main Street in our little farming community. In those days, a status symbol for men and boys alike was to carry a jackknife. But after I suffered a deep cut on my finger, my father forbade me from having a knife of my own until I was older. My lack of a pocket knife relegated me to second class among my peers. But one warm summer day this changed.

Meeting a friend on Main Street, I noticed something in his pocket. "What's that?" I asked.

"My knife," he replied, trying to lower his voice to emulate adult authority. "Do you want to see it?"

"You bet!" I replied, immediately holding out my hand. "Is it sharp?"

"I don't know," he answered. "The blade is rusted shut so I haven't been able to open it for a long time."

Now the wheels of my mind were turning. I could carry this knife for status without disobeying my father. "Could I borrow it for a while?" I asked hesitantly.

"Sure. In fact, you can keep it," replied my friend. "I have another one that really cuts."

"How long can I have it?"

"It's yours *for keeps,*" he told me.

"For keeps?" I asked, staring at my new treasure.

"Yes, for keeps," he reassured me.

That word *keeps* made the knife mine permanently. When something is yours for keeps, it really belongs to you. Look to your spouse and realize that this person, given to you by God, is yours in a very special way—for keeps!

FAITHFULNESS: FORSAKING ALL OTHERS

The vow "forsaking all others" answers the question of the third-party affair. You clearly stated there would be no one else for the rest of your life. At the time, when your relationship was new and fresh, forsaking others was an easy task. But *you promised* to continue to forsake others and to love one another day after day, month after month, year after year, "so long as you both shall live."

No one is above temptation, but the Bible gives clear direction on what to do when tempted. The apostle Paul told young Timothy, "Flee also youthful lusts; but pursue righteousness, faith, love, peace with those who call on the Lord out of a pure heart."[4] We are told not to *casually avoid,* but to *boldly run* from evil. This lesson is demonstrated in the Bible when Potiphar's wife attempted to seduce young, handsome Joseph:

> But it happened about this time, when Joseph went into the house to do his work, and none of the men of the house was inside, that she caught him by his garment, saying, "Lie with me." But he left his garment in her hand, and fled and ran outside.[5]

In order to remain faithful to one, there are times when you must literally run from the temptation of others.

Please note one other subtle point in these two examples. If Timothy and Joseph were obedient by running or fleeing temptation, then surely they must have *felt* the temptation. The lesson is this: *The problem is not the feelings that accompany temptation, but rather our behavior in response to those feelings*. Behavior and feelings are often confused as being the same, when actually they are very different.

Feelings are involuntary emotional responses to a situation. They are neither good nor bad, but they are real. Behavior is an action response to a feeling. The Bible tells us how to respond to a given feeling. In this situation we are told to flee, run, or get away from the temptation as quickly as possible.

Somehow we who call ourselves evangelical Christians have all but forgotten perseverance in the commitments we have made. Vows and covenants are no longer chic in our modern theology. Only God makes promises, not us. This same mentality has influenced the way many Christians do business. Time and again I have heard people say, "I'd rather do business with a non-Christian any day; unbelievers are more dependable."

You may try to rationalize your search for greener pastures. I have heard many reasons in my office, and some are very convincing. But whatever your reasons, there is one fact you cannot rationalize away. *You gave your word. You promised* to "forsake all others for as long as you both shall live." God will hold you to it.

UNCONDITIONAL COMMITMENT, FROM THIS DAY FORWARD

Then you said:

> I, ____________________, take thee ____________________ to be my wedded husband/wife, to have and to hold from this day forward, for better, for worse, for richer, for poorer, in sickness and in health, to love and to cherish, till death us do part.[6]

Judy always smiles as she recalls this portion of the vows. In spite of all my rehearsing earlier in the day on the barn roof, I still managed to leave out "in sickness" as I repeated the words from memory.

After I had finished, she quietly whispered, "You forgot to say 'in sickness.'"

Without a ruffle I quietly replied, "That too!"

We both joke now that the omission must have had a positive effect on her health. At age sixteen she was flat on her back for six months with a severe case of rheumatic fever. At that time the doctor told her she would always have to take things easy and learn to watch the rest of the world go by. Since we have been married, however, she has given birth to our three children and runs a very busy household, including (voluntarily!) cutting the grass in the summer and clearing the driveway of snow in the winter.

For Better, for Worse

Here we have two unlimited extremes. Believe it or not, "for better" should not be passed over lightly. There are unique temptations when things are "better." Laziness, complacency, and boredom can enter, bringing about decay in the relationship. These factors often result from success and the abundance of comfort. I am sure you can think of a couple who shocked you by getting a divorce. The typical comment is, "They seemed so happy and had everything going for them." Remember, there are subtle hazards in the "for better" part of your marriage.

What are the limits of "for worse"? This is the question I am often asked by persons in marital difficulty. According to the vows you made, the "for worse" is not qualified or limited in any way. "That's not fair. We didn't know what we were getting into at the time," some complain. Nevertheless, if you decide to end your marriage because the relationship is "for worse," you must abandon your vows and break your promise.

One Christian man who has given his life to propagating the gospel and who seriously flirted with leaving his wife and family, gives pointed advice to those who excuse themselves with past misjudgments: "Stop blaming your past for your present condition: accept responsibility for your own behavior. Most things that we don't like about ourselves *can* be changed with God's help."

That's no platitude! He and his wife, giving the glory to Jesus Christ, did just that. In the face of difficulties, which had been building up since the beginning of their marriage, they turned from their hardness to one another and have made their "for worse" better!

For Richer, for Poorer

Money is a subject everyone relates to. Most people do not have "enough." But when the question comes up, "How much do we need?" the universal reply seems to be, "Just a little bit more." Most of us can identify with this condition. But wealth can also bring problems. The Scriptures teach that the love of money is the root of all evil.

A young wife with whom I counseled came into my office one day with a new problem. "I'm worried because my husband feels he has to earn seven-and-a-half million dollars before he can let up," she said.

Her concern was not without grounds. Her husband was a successful businessman who had already nearly earned his first million. She explained that his figures showed he must have over seven million dollars before he could be financially independent. For this woman, "for richer" was squeezing her out of his life.

Having counseled with several wealthy couples, I have learned about other hazards that accompany the "for richer" category. These couples often find their wealth takes more and more control of them instead of them controlling their wealth. Their world revolves around the making and spending of money. In these situations, I often recall the words of James:

> Come now, you who say, "Today or tomorrow we will go to such and such a city, spend a year there, buy and sell, and make a profit"; whereas you do not know what will happen tomorrow. For what is your life? It is even a vapor that appears for a little time and then vanishes away.[7]

Because of their money, the rich seem to need each other less. The personal attention and services given and received by the spouses in most wealthy marriages are often purchased. The cook prepares the meals, the gardener does the yard, the secretary buys the gifts, and the party is provided by the country club. In a later chapter you will learn how relationships are built on meeting one another's needs.

When the satisfaction of needs is *purchased,* the relationship is formed with the money rather than with the spouse.

"For poorer" is the category most of us identify with. Our response depends largely upon *when* in the marriage we are poor. In the early stages it is acceptable. You may still be in school, new in your job, starting your own business, or making other preparations for your career. *You have not yet had a chance to fail.*

In our society of free enterprise, the possession of material goods implies having money. Money indicates earning power, which symbolizes success. Therefore, the more years you add to your marriage the more difficult it will become to remain contented in the "for poorer" group. But in your vows, the "for poorer" was not qualified—it may mean "for poorer" until death us do part!

In Sickness and in Health

"She has had seven major surgeries and spent the majority of the last ten years in and out of hospitals. Many of these illnesses were unrelated and, as she would recover from one, another would develop. Holidays were frequently celebrated in a hospital room and their growing son's achievements were reported secondhand by her husband. At the end of all this, she is still not well. Most of her illnesses are chronic, and she has been told by doctors that she will have to learn to live with the pain and discomfort. Nothing more can be done."

A disheartening report to be sure. But these two Christians are living out their vows "to love and to cherish in sickness . . . till death us do part." Today they are more in love than ever before. Interested friends have asked them if they ever get discouraged in the midst of their trials.

"More than you will ever know," they respond. "But we have learned to express our anger and negative feelings toward the illness and not toward the person who is ill."

How easy it is for a chronically ill person to feel guilty because of his illness, the trouble he causes other people, and his lack of response to treatment. Any negative feelings expressed by the healthy spouse regarding the illness are often taken personally, thus feeding the guilt.

Remember that your body is the temple of the Holy Spirit. Whether your body is sick or healthy, the Holy Spirit lives within you.

Here is what Scripture tells us:

> Or do you not know that your body is the temple of the Holy Spirit who is in you, whom you have from God, and you are not your own? For you were bought at a price; therefore glorify God in your body and in your spirit, which are God's.[8]

The Holy Spirit dwells within the body of the Christian. He is present regardless of your physical health. God has promised this unconditionally. In like manner you made the same promise in your wedding vows: "to love and to cherish in *sickness* and in health till death us do part."

One day I asked this same couple why they were so close and so much in love. As they were pondering their response, I specifically asked the husband why he had never divorced his wife. His response was simple but profound: "Well, after all, we *are* married and she *is* my wife." They had made a promise they intended to keep!

Several days later I saw them again, and the wife said that after thinking about my question she had finally concluded that their marriage was founded not on romantic love but on a carefully developed intimacy. "Romantic love is there," she said, "but it comes and goes with the moods of the situation. It is the intimacy of deeply knowing each other and unconditionally accepting each other that really forms the basis of our relationship."

Then *I* had to think about *her* comment for several days. Previously, I had thought it must be the patience and understanding they tried to maintain toward each other through these trying years that kept them going. But that was not it at all. Rather it was the freedom to show the pain, depression, extreme anger, frustration, and giving up on everything only to hope again. It was this *freedom* of honest expression of all the *feelings* and *thoughts*—especially the negative, unpleasant ones—in which the seeds of intimacy were planted and grew into a strong marriage relationship. Although her body was sick and weak, their relationship was strong and healthy, filled with beauty and life.

Whether you experience illness or job failure or obesity, you can develop with this same process an intimacy that provides the strong foundation for your marriage.

To Love and to Cherish

The phrase *to love and to cherish* introduces another word that is seldom a part of our daily vocabulary. We have already discussed the word, *love*. But what about *cherish?* What is the meaning of the promise to cherish our partner?

In my college classroom, where pearls of wisdom always came forth from students at unexpected times, I learned an important lesson on the meaning of this word. I asked the class what they thought about when they considered the word *cherish*. One guy in the back row of the lecture hall shouted, "My 1957 Chevrolet!"

"I'm looking for serious answers," I replied.

"This one is serious," he retorted.

We then listened as he proceeded to teach us a lesson on cherishing. He told about his "prize baby," the 1957 four-door Chevrolet sedan he had acquired in high school. Anyone familiar with cars of this vintage knows they have become classics. The young man rented a special garage to house the car. "I keep it immaculately clean, rubbing out any sign of rust before it appears to the naked eye, and I only drive the car in nice weather. There is absolutely nothing within my means that I wouldn't do or spend to care for my car."

That's it! I thought. *If everyone could just think of and treat their spouse the same way this fellow did his car, cherishing would be a real part of marriage.*

Is it becoming clear why your vows are so important? Intimacy, the foundation of a relationship, cannot develop unless you are truly free to be yourself. And you cannot be yourself unless you know your partner unconditionally accepts you and will always be there.

So Long as You Both Shall Live

Marriage is a *lifetime* proposition. Anything less than that is not God's way. In Genesis we are told, "Therefore a man shall leave his father and mother and be joined to his wife, and they shall become one flesh."[9]

The man and woman do not become "as one" or "similar to being one," but indeed *are* one flesh. This is a new entity, a shared human nature, a creation ordained by God and compared to the love relationship of all love relationships, Christ and the church. To experience what the intimacy of marriage really is, your promise must be unconditional—which means it is for a lifetime.

Many young couples today are revising their vows. One of the more common revisions is, as we have noted, to replace the word *live* with *love*. The vows then read, "so long as we both shall love." That simple change of one small word completely alters what you promise. It makes a conditional promise out of one that must be unconditional. What you are saying is that your promise holds true only as long as you are aware of a love for your partner.

Anyone who has been married a few years knows that romantic love waxes and wanes amidst the constant changes of an intimate relationship. In the heat of an argument, the feelings of romantic love often become confused and distorted. *Conditional vows plant a seed of insecurity right from the beginning.*

Lack of commitment and the *deterioration of a relationship* go hand in hand. While sitting in group therapy one night, someone noticed that only one person in the entire group was wearing a wedding ring. Being the therapist in the group, I wished I had been perceptive enough to make that observation. However, it was significant that a group member who was not wearing a ring pointed it out to the rest of us.

The group picked up on it and through discussion learned

that each person had a definite reason for removing the ring. Every one of them reflected on a time when they began to withdraw trust and commitment from the other. (Incidentally, the one person wearing his ring was a husband who had expressed a certainty of his love for his wife and was trying, without doubt, to save his marriage. He was committed to her.) The lesson here is that the absence of commitment, sometimes symbolized by the absence of wedding rings, is a common denominator for most couples having marital problems.

Try to recall those moments *after* your vows were said. You were probably wearing a shiny, new wedding ring. Your spouse probably had to have your help in putting it on your finger during the ceremony. Or if you were like me, you left it stuck halfway on your finger until the pastor prayed. Then when no one was looking, you slipped it on the rest of the way.

After the benediction, the church bells rang and you turned around, arm in arm with your spouse, to face the congregation and the world. For the first time you heard yours names officially Mr. and Mrs. when the pastor introduced you. And then it seemed like the longest moment in history from the pastor's pronouncement until the organist started the recessional.

Can you remember—or better yet—*relive* in your heart the feelings you shared as you hurried up the aisle as husband and wife? I trust that, as with us, your joy was complete, for your commitment was fresh and full of meaning. The knot had been tied not only at the church but also in heaven.

Chapter Four

God Designed You Not to Be Alone

A single glance into the waiting room was sufficient to identify the person I would be seeing for the first time in counseling that morning. His newness to this situation was evident as he tried to blend in with the regulars who had been coming weeks, months, and even years.

To most people this tall, well-dressed businessman appeared impeccable in every respect, even down to his well-trimmed, slightly graying mustache. But to those of us who are experienced in inviting people from the waiting room into our offices, he gave himself away. He held an outdated magazine from the nearby table, flipping the pages as though he were intensely interested. His eyes, however, seemed to look at everything in the room except the pages before him. They moved quickly from face to face so as not to appear as though he were staring at the others. Yet silently he seemed to be asking himself, *I wonder why they are here?*

Almost as a conditioned response, he vaulted to his feet when he heard me call his name and charged toward me with his hand extended. He displayed a false confidence I am certain he had practiced for years as a sales executive. What he did not realize was that in his other hand he was still clutching the magazine that had been his security during the wait.

Taking the chair closest to the door in my office, he sat down and with a slight twinge of embarrassment laid the magazine on the floor beside him. Sitting silently, I allowed him to settle into the quiet privacy of the office. He seemed relieved to be there but anxious about where all this therapy might lead. In only a matter of moments his well-developed defenses began to disappear. The confident, aggressive businessman gradually transformed into a frightened, insecure person, showing traces of panic across his face.

I let my eyes do the talking as I patiently waited for his first words. In a barely audible whisper he said, "I don't know who I really am." His eyes moved slowly from the floor in front of him to the window and a small lake behind the clinic. In a slightly stronger voice, but still preoccupied in his thoughts, he continued, "I don't even know what I am like." Then, realizing that I was in the room with him, his eyes searched mine as he said, "I feel I'm all alone."

This gentleman seemed to have everything a man could want. He was married and had three healthy children and a successful, growing business. He and his family had recently moved into a new house and had it furnished by a professional decorator. He had all the evidences of success. Yet he was searching.

"I know what I need," he finally said near the close of our session.

"What?" I asked, hoping he was sensing what had become apparent to me.

"I need a close personal relationship," he replied.

It seemed as if he should have had several, but in the demands of his business lifestyle he had always set them aside. Now it was catching up with him. In the sessions that followed I worked with him as he successfully developed his personal relationships, beginning with his wife.

THE NEED FOR RELATIONSHIPS

What this man discovered to be his basic need is not unique to him. We all need at least one close personal relationship, and much of our activity and behavior is centered on finding and maintaining that relationship. For most of us this relationship is ideally found in our marriage, but for some it is found elsewhere.

For some of you it may be God's will that you remain single. Others of you have become single through the death of your spouse. But whether or not you are married, everyone needs to have at least one close personal relationship. If you do not, you will have a sense of loneliness.

Loneliness, the absence of relationships, can hurt you physically as well as emotionally. Relationships are essential to your physical health. Dr. James J. Lynch, a specialist in psychosomatic medicine, tells us that the absence of relationships brings emotional and then physical deterioration. Human touch and caring has a profound effect on a person's recovery from illness. He further points out that doctors and others must make people aware that family life is as important to health as is diet and exercise. Without question, Dr. Lynch reports, there is a biological basis for our need to form human relationships, and if we fail to fulfill that need, our health is in peril.[1] Let's face it: we need relationships to survive.

This is why divorced people tell of being so incredibly lonely. They have known the intimacy of a warm, close relationship and now it exists no longer. The emptiness and hollowness that come after a divorce can be devastating.

One newly divorced man, an active and productive Christian, wrote, "I yearn to come home to a house that is a home—full of life and love and laughter. Instead, my house is empty, my bed is cold. My children no longer come home to me. I find it extremely difficult to admit that my family will never be back together again, that my children will never live with me, and that I will possibly have to live alone the rest of my life."

As we examine why Christian marriages are failing, we need to know why people choose to get married in the first place. What motivates someone to marry? What motivates people to leave a life of singleness and independence to enter a relationship for a lifetime? What leads people to accept the controls, limits, and expectations that are placed on them by another person, another family, and by society as a whole?

I believe the answer lies in the importance of relationships in our lives. At the risk of becoming too theoretical, I would like to spend the remainder of this chapter showing you exactly how much your relationships mean to you. Please stay with me, for the principles I am about to discuss will be the foundation for the rest of the book.

REVEALING WHO YOU ARE

Through relationships you find answers to the questions "Who am I?" and "What am I like?" The relationships you have and your ability to form the ones you need are the keys to finding your self-identity and self-esteem. You cannot know who you are or how you feel about yourself without having an understanding of how other people see you.

You determine what you are like by how others perceive you. The presence or the addition of new relationships creates happiness and usually a good self-concept. On the other hand, their absence or loss brings about dejection and a loss of self-worth.

This truth was vividly illustrated to me years ago by my daughter, Leah, who is just six years old. (Children are great teachers. Their feelings are still right on the surface. They have not yet had the opportunity to develop sophisticated defensive systems to cover their true emotions.)

This particular afternoon Leah came into the house in tears. She was crying so hard that I was certain she had been seriously hurt. I met Judy at the kitchen door, and as we dashed to her rescue we asked simultaneously, "Leah, what happened?"

Relieved at first at the absence of any scrapes or blood, we listened intently as she blurted out between sobs, "I have no friends. No one will play with me."

The tears streaming down her face and her sobs made us realize her hurt was more severe than two skinned knees *and* a bump on the head. Her hurt feelings were right there where everyone could see them and respond. I held her closely, reassuring her that I would be her friend. Two hours later, Leah was walking through the house, laughing and singing with two friends behind her. But I wondered about all the kids we call adults, all over the world today, who are crying like Leah because they have no friends. Of course, their sobs are carefully hidden behind cosmetic smiles, safely out of the reach of anyone who might respond.

MEETING YOUR BASIC NEEDS

Not only are relationships important in discovering who you are, they also play a vital role in meeting your basic needs. What are these basic needs? Dr. William Glasser, a psychiatrist and founder of reality therapy, defines them as (1) to love and be loved and (2) to feel worthwhile to yourself and others.[2]

According to Dr. Glasser, all our behavior revolves around these two basic emotional needs. One logical conclusion can be drawn from this principle: Relationships are required to meet these needs. Only then will you experience loving, being loved, and knowing that you are indeed worthwhile.

Your relationships are formed and sustained by what I call a "mutual need-meeting activity." Think of a relationship that you have and examine how it formed and what keeps it going. In the beginning you met some of this person's needs, and in turn he or she met some of yours. The more needs that are successfully met, the stronger the relationship becomes. In contrast, the fewer the needs that are met in both directions, the weaker the relationship becomes. If you become skillful in responding to the needs of others, I guarantee that you will have relationships.

Let me emphasize here that by need-meeting I do not mean a selfish, self-centered stance where you are out for what you can get. Rather, it starts as an expression of giving. After all, the Bible teaches us that giving produces greater happiness than receiving.[3] But as you begin giving to someone, it is natural for them to give in return. When this happens you have a relationship. When it doesn't, a relationship will not form. If there was one, it will not continue, but will weaken and fall apart. The same is true in your marriage.

Here is an example of how this worked for us with our neighbors. One family in our neighborhood seemed to have almost every material possession a family could ever want.

Our friendship was cordial, but not particularly close. Then one fall day as we were putting away our summer yard equipment, I noticed my neighbor had a need I could meet. He had a paddle boat that needed to be stored for the winter, and I had the storage space.

By storing his boat for him, a series of exchanges was begun whereby we have both benefited from the other's favors, and our relationship has been strengthened. Obviously, the relationship is really built on the emotional needs that are met in the process of our doing favors for each other.

You cannot fully understand your human relationships until you have a relationship with God, your Creator. God wants and invites us to have a relationship with Him.

The Old Testament prophet recorded about God's Word: "For I desire mercy and not sacrifice, / And the knowledge of God more than burnt offerings."[4] The message could not have been clearer. At a time in Israel's history when sacrifices and offerings had degenerated into mere form, God rejected them and called His people back to a relationship with Him. His priority is clear. God wants our love. He wants us to know Him. Furthermore, He wants us to love one another as He has loved us.[5]

THE RELATIONSHIP OF A LIFETIME

Most relationships do not last for a lifetime. New ones form and others end. Those relationships that do last go through many stages. However, when a relationship changes it has an emotional effect upon you. Usually your strongest feelings are directly connected to the beginning or ending of a relationship. You change jobs. You move to a new neighborhood. Parents die. Children grow up. Relationships continue to change.

In the midst of all this you need a constant, stable relationship to carry you through a lifetime of changes—one that remains constant when everything else seems to be in a state of flux.

A responsive, constant marriage relationship provides confidence, stability, and security. When everything else lets you down, your marriage assures you that you are loved and worthwhile to at least one person—your marriage partner. If you are not married and God wills for you to remain single, this relationship will be provided in some other form. On the other hand, if you are married and the relationship is failing, you can see how the very foundation of your stability is being shaken.

In the United States today, about 95 percent of all men and women marry.[6] In spite of the problems the institution of marriage is facing in our society, it is fascinating to see that people still prefer a lifestyle of marriage as opposed to singleness.

What is even more astonishing is that most people who experience marriage failure and divorce choose to try again. Of all the women under forty who divorce, 90 percent eventually remarry. And divorced men are more likely to remarry than divorced women.[7] My point here is not to deal with the question of remarriage, but to show that most people have a strong need for the constant, committed relationship of marriage even though they may have previously failed at it.

MEANT TO BE MARRIED

I believe that God intends almost everyone to be married, including Carol, who has a happy ending to a story filled with problems. She first came to me after seeing her family doctor because she had been experiencing some strange physical symptoms—double vision and numbness in her feet.

After undergoing a variety of neurological tests, this attractive, energetic young nurse was told that she had multiple sclerosis, a chronic disease of the nervous system often resulting in increased physical disability. Many people with this malady end up in a wheelchair with varying degrees of paralysis. For others, the symptoms remain minimal for years. Since this was Carol's situation, she could continue working as a nursing instructor.

To my surprise, when I talked with Carol in that initial session she said she was accepting the illness just fine. It was her marriage that she could not figure out. Her husband had withdrawn and was becoming more distant and noncommunicative. In one brief session with him alone, he told me he wanted a divorce and made it clear he was not interested in marriage counseling. His reasons for wanting to end the marriage were vague, puzzling both Carol and me. Because of the timing of his decision, however, I was led to believe he was running scared and afraid of spending a lifetime with an invalid wife.

He did leave her. My contacts with Carol continued over the years, helping her cope with the single life she had never wanted nor asked for.

Not long ago I received one of those telephone calls that leaves anyone in my business in total suspense. The call was from Carol. With a puzzled excitement she said, "Jerry, you will never guess what is happening to me!"

I searched frantically for the appropriate reply, but unable to wait for a response, she blurted out, "I'm getting married!" Trying to remain professional, yet elated with the news, I agreed to meet with them before they tied the knot.

The session was a beautiful experience. Rarely do I find myself meeting with couples who are happy and very much in love. Carol's future husband, who had never been married, was a doctor trained in the specialty of physical medicine, which would be extremely helpful to Carol. As they were leaving my office, Carol turned to me with a glow of happiness on her face that I had never seen before and said, "Let's face it, Jerry. I was just meant to be married!"

I thought, *Yes, Carol, you and almost everyone else.*

THE MARITAL DEPENDENCY INDICATOR[8]

Is the dependency you have toward your partner healthy or unhealthy? Take this test for a quick indicator as to whether this area of your relationship needs special attention.

Please circle the number that correlates most closely to your true response. (1) Strongly disagree, (2) disagree, (3) undecided, (4) agree, (5) strongly agree.

1. I sense rejection when my partner is away for a period of time.	1	2	3	4	5
2. Important personal decisions are discussed with my partner before making them.	1	2	3	4	5
3. When my partner is unhappy, I usually feel I am responsible even before we discuss it.	1	2	3	4	5
4. I go to my partner with my personal feelings of fear and inadequacy.	1	2	3	4	5
5. At social gatherings I always need to be near my partner.	1	2	3	4	5
6. When disagreements occur, I tend to agree with my partner rather than experience conflict.	1	2	3	4	5
7. I rely on my partner's strengths for support in areas of my personal weakness.	1	2	3	4	5
8. I need my partner to understand our financial situation with me.	1	2	3	4	5
9. I am threatened by my partner's friendships with others.	1	2	3	4	5
10. I prefer my partner decline social engagements for us.	1	2	3	4	5
11. I am comfortable letting my partner see me cry.	1	2	3	4	5
12. I feel I cannot express my true feelings when I am upset.	1	2	3	4	5
13. I love to be pampered when I am ill.	1	2	3	4	5
14. When my partner lets me down, I immediately go back to my parents for support.	1	2	3	4	5

15. I derive more satisfaction from giving affection than receiving it.	1 2 3 4 5
16. I am always hurt when my partner does not like what I am wearing.	1 2 3 4 5
17. I feel guilty when I enjoy doing a leisure activity without my partner.	1 2 3 4 5
18. In athletic competition, I enjoy seeing my partner win against everyone but me.	1 2 3 4 5
19. In social situations, I tend to correct my partner's comments when they are inaccurate.	1 2 3 4 5
20. I will do almost anything to please my partner, even take this dependency indicator test.	1 2 3 4 5

Scoring Instructions

Total the number of all the questions to determine your overall independency/dependency test score.

INDEPENDENT/DEPENDENT FACTOR

Independent: Able to derive satisfaction and fulfillment without the involvement of another person.

Dependent: Satisfaction and fulfillment is related to the factor of involvement with another person based upon needing and being needed.

(20–40)---------------------*Strongly independent*
(41–60)---------------------*Moderately independent*
(61–80)---------------------*Moderately dependent*
(81–100)-------------------*Strongly dependent*

HEALTHY DEPENDENCY

Healthy Dependency: The needing and being needed process contributes to the bonding and smooth functioning of the relationship.

Total the numbers from questions (2,4,7,8,11,13,15,18, 20) to determine your Healthy Dependency Score.

(9–18)----------------------*No dependency*
(19–27)----------------------*Some dependency*
(28–36)----------------------*Moderately dependent*
(37–45)----------------------*Strongly dependent*

UNHEALTHY DEPENDENCY

Unhealthy Dependency: The needing and being needed process creates a sense of stress from undesirable control or obligation on the part of one partner to the other.

Total the numbers from questions (1,3,5,6,9,10,12,14,16, 17,19) to determine your Unhealthy Dependency Score.

(11–22)---------------------*None*
(23–33)---------------------*Some possible*
(34–44)---------------------*Moderately dependent*
(45–55)---------------------*Strongly dependent*

The uniqueness of each couple needs to be considered with respect to the questions. However, if your Unhealthy Dependency Score falls within the moderately dependent range, you should examine more closely your dependency patterns. Determine if you sense unwanted pressures from your partner. If so, discuss ways of changing attitudes and behavior to alleviate this unwelcome dependency. If your Unhealthy Dependency score falls within the strongly dependent range or if you cannot resolve unwelcome dependency patterns under your own efforts, we recommend that you explore your marital dependency patterns with a qualified marriage counselor.

Chapter Five

Too Good to Be Real

Many Christian husbands and wives are strangers to each other. As we saw in the last chapter, they have never allowed their marriage to become the truly intimate relationship it was intended to be. Having previously experienced rejection when their negative side was revealed to others, they have chosen in their marriage to disclose only the good part of themselves. It is easy to show patience, kindness, self-confidence, and other traits that successfully pass the acceptance test of others while safely concealing fears, anger, insecurities, and other negative traits behind defensive walls, out of the reach of their partners.

I'll never forget the shock I encountered when a couple who were my close Christian friends announced they were getting a divorce. They were in their midthirties and for years had hosted an exciting Bible study in their home. In fact, the group had become so large, and so many people had made professions of faith in Jesus Christ, that they had had a huge room built on the back of the house just to hold everyone.

This couple was, as they say in the South, part of the "blue blood" of the city. Both were from prominent families. She had been a beauty queen; he was repeatedly elected to state government posts. In these capacities, they had both borne consistent verbal witness.

When the news of the divorce became public, I had a chance to visit with the wife and ask her why. She told me that she and her husband had always been at the top of everything they had ever tried to do. He loved her award-winning beauty; she saw him as her ideal public leader and spiritual stalwart. But their relationship had never grown. When she probed her mind to produce a one-sentence answer to my question, she said, "I guess we fell in love with each other's image."

Their marriage, the burgeoning study group and, you guessed it, even a number of the new converts all went down the drain.

YOUR BEST ISN'T EVERYTHING

Showing your good characteristics and concealing your negative ones is a pattern that starts early in life. From infancy you are taught to do this both in what you are told and in what you see other people do. One of those early messages may have been, "Be careful what you do. What will people think?" As you became skillful at determining what people thought, you learned that they liked your good characteristics and rejected your negative feelings in various ways.

If you are like most of us, this message was repeated over and over throughout your childhood until you were grown up and no one needed to tell you anymore. You now have a recording of the voice in your head, and it plays all by itself, even when you wish it would not.

This pattern of concealing negative feelings can become so integrated into your behavior that you are unaware you're doing it. Others will notice something is lacking in your relationships, but they won't know what it is. You are allowing others to relate to only a *part* of you—the good part. And that is *too good to be real*.

Concealing your negative feelings is not always bad. Relationships among single people are never intended to handle that level of openness. I have counseled with many single persons who have revealed too much of themselves too quickly, resulting in hurt and rejection. Your personality defenses that cover your needs and feelings protect your self-esteem as a relationship is being formed. One of the exciting aspects of a new relationship is watching it grow as each person progressively divulges more and more of himself or herself.

Marriage, however, is a different story. Since it is intended to be the most intimate of all relationships, you must know all of your partner—the good and the bad. For many this is a difficult task. They would rather expose only their good side, knowing that by doing this acceptance is guaranteed. After all, that is what they were taught and it has worked in other relationships for years. Although it will also work in marriage, by sharing only a part of yourself you are seriously limiting the relationship and creating a superficial marriage.

In this superficial relationship you will talk comfortably about the neighbors, your job, world events, almost anything as long as you stay away from discussing each other. "We-talk," as some of my couples have come to call it, is more difficult. That deeper level of communication leads to private material in yourself that has been tucked away for years. We-talk does not come easily, but the positive effect on your relationship will make it worth the effort.

One Christian minister, whose shaky marriage was being restored, advised: "Take time to get to know about your mate's past. Hold nothing back, or if anything is held back, assume personal responsibility that what is being held back is not detrimental to a good understanding of yourself by your mate. Find out what things in the past hurt, felt good, and brought hope. Start immediately to learn how to discuss ideas and feelings in an accepting, noncondemning frame of reference."

He continued, "I would not have allowed my wife's feelings of insecurity to go unchallenged and untreated for as long as I did. Being 'patient' in that way with a mate is not good for them. They need to work toward changes in their lives of those things that are detrimental to the marriage.

"I would have learned better ways to explain why I am the person I am. I would have tried harder to communicate on a feelings level instead of descending into the same old circular arguments on the basis of cold facts! 'You did! I didn't! Yes, you did! No, I didn't,' etc."

More than anyone else, the Christian has the potential to be open and honest with his feelings. Yet I have found the opposite to be true. Growing up as one committed to Christ and knowing many who love the Lord, I have come to realize that we are conditioned even more than others to keep our negatives concealed. We have an obsessive preoccupation with how we appear to others. If we have a problem or need that may reflect failure or weakness, especially in our faith, our first concern is not to resolve the problem but, instead to make sure that no one finds out.

LOVING BEHAVIOR, THE RESULT OF INTIMACY

Why are Christians, more than other people, likely to appear *too good to be real?* Because, in reality, they are! Look at what God's Word tells us about perfection. "For by one offering He has perfected forever all those who are being sanctified."[1]

Theologians tell us this verse points out that in the eyes of God we are indeed perfect. However, let us remember that we are perfected by a single offering, the shed blood of Jesus Christ, the Son of God. God sees us as perfect through His Son. Therefore, our perfection is based on *our relationship with the Lord,* not on *what we do*. Our Christian behavior is not the source of our perfection; it is the result of it.

Both our Christian behavior and our loving relationship with God are important, but we tend to get the order reversed. After we have become aware of God's love for us, an open, honest relationship of faith and trust must come first. The behavior follows as a natural response to that relationship.

The same is true in your marriage. The relationship of love and trust must be established first. Then loving behavior follows as a natural response to that firmly established intimate relationship. This will happen only as you get to know more about each other. Your partner is allowed the opportunity to accept and understand some intimate parts of yourself that you were sure he or she would reject.

I remember a couple who encountered this situation. The silence was heavy between each word spoken by a guilty wife. Her husband had reassured her of his love, but she had not tested it until now, as she unfolded a story about herself that she was certain would lead to his rejecting her.

But it didn't. He listened with care, and after she finished, she broke into tears and threw herself into his arms. They had not physically demonstrated their affection for months, but now the love expressed verbally had been tested. An intimate relationship was firmly established and loving behavior naturally followed.

As a way of avoiding their needs and feelings during those first sessions, most couples I see tend to focus on the other's behavior, or on "who does what." By the time they come to see me, they are often tired of doing all those good things that are unappreciated by their partner. Finally becoming fed up, they decide it is time to expect something in return. They come to me, expecting a referee or negotiator with the wisdom to offer supreme fairness.

At first they continue to spar with each other, pointing out all the good they give to the relationship and the little they receive from it. What they are doing is avoiding their real needs and feelings about themselves and each other.

Often couples become irritated with me because, in spite of all my professional wisdom, I do not come up with the decree as to who should carry out the garbage. However, as the sessions progress the focus moves from surface issues to removing the walls and showing the feelings they were sure would never be understood. Often to the couple's surprise, as emotions are shared and not rejected, the garbage somehow seems to get carried out—usually by the one who walks through the kitchen and notices that the container is full!

A marriage relationship is not built on negotiated behavior, but rather on intimacy that develops from communicating emotional needs and feelings, both the good and the negative ones.

THE VICIOUS CYCLE OF HOSTILITY AND DEFENSIVENESS

How does it affect you when you're around someone you care about and they will not let you get close to them? You probably find that you become impatient and then downright angry. Hostility and defensiveness go hand in hand. One person's defensiveness brings out hostility in another person.

You can always count on people in a therapy group to react honestly to each other. Predictably, anger is kindled in the members when one of them becomes defensive and shuts out the rest of the group.

As a matter of fact, I must often deal with anger in myself as I counsel with a defensive person. I have concluded that a person's defensiveness is essentially a rejection of *you*. The defensive person does to you exactly what they are afraid you will do to them. Their defensiveness tells you that they do not trust you or your response to what they might reveal. Actually, you are being shut out.

Can you see what this does in a marriage? If the husband, for example, is defensive about some feelings, his wife will begin to get angry and feel shut out. Threatened by his wife's anger, his natural response is to close off even further, which in turn causes his wife to become even more angry. The process is a vicious downward spiral that often ends in a violent argument or total withdrawal.

This cause-and-effect process of defensiveness and anger is one of the most common problems in Christian marriages. Its basis is in the initial decision of one of the partners not to be open with some needs or feelings that are necessary for the relationship to grow. And I believe *this all goes back to Christians viewing perfection as never sinning, instead of seeing perfection as the ability to receive forgiveness in the pursuit of righteousness*.

HONESTY: THE BEGINNING OF TRUST

Early one Monday morning I received a telephone call from a pastor in our community. I knew this man quite well and routinely saw referrals from him. This time he presented a different situation.

The couple he was calling about were strangers. They had chosen not to go to their own pastor, fearing his knowledge of their problems. They had carefully selected someone from the other side of the city. Furthermore, they wanted to meet with a Christian counselor who did not know their pastor or the people from their church.

Because I met these qualifications, he asked if I would be willing to counsel them. Even though I had not met them, I already sensed in myself some resentment toward their defensiveness. However, as a favor to my pastor friend and because of my commitment to see any couple for at least one session, I reluctantly scheduled their first appointment.

When they arrived, it was even worse than I had anticipated. As I picked up the file containing general information that we obtain from all referrals, my receptionist said, "Good luck. I'm glad it's you and not I who's meeting with them!" It was a significant comment, for her patience and tolerance almost never allows her to make such a caustic statement unless someone has really given her a hard time.

Observing this couple through the glass in the waiting-room door, I saw two tense, hostile people sitting in opposite corners of the room, like fighters in a ring, awaiting the bell to begin round one. I would not have known they were together had they not been the only two persons in the room.

Taking a deep breath, I cleared my throat, opened the door, and called their names. From the far corner of the room, the husband darted toward me as if he were racing his wife, though he never once glanced at her. As he approached, he asked curtly, "Which office?"

Almost as a natural reflex I replied, "First one on the left." He went by me as if he worked there and disappeared into my office.

Meanwhile, I was still standing there holding open the door for his wife, who seemed to be deliberately taking her time gathering up her purse, sweater, two books, and a tablet with what appeared to be a list of grievances regarding her husband. She said nothing as she stood rigidly and started toward me. Her face was strained, her lips drawn so tightly together that her mouth appeared permanently sealed shut.

As she passed me at the door her stone face shifted to a forced smile—one of those courtesy gestures—that seemed to be a major effort. The smile was so brief that I am certain I would have missed it had I blinked. I took one last glance at my receptionist, whose reassuring look told me she would remain no matter what happened during the next hour.

As I closed the door and sat down, I saw two tightly coiled springs ready to be released. They watched me as if they expected me to fire the starting gun to open their verbal contest. The gun went off when I said, "Who would like to tell me why you are here?"

The husband won the start by saying he would go first, and without wasting a breath he began his list of complaints about what his wife did not do for the marriage, at the same time emphasizing how hard he was trying. He got no further than the second point when his wife began interrupting with denials and clarifications on each of his accusations. While reclarifying her clarifications, confusion hit and they were into one of their inevitable, nonproductive fights.

Between the shouts and the tears there was a lull. This was my moment. Profoundly I declared that it was certainly clear to me that they needed to be there, with which they both agreed. (If you can get people like this to agree on anything, I consider it progress. Besides, that safe statement kept me in a neutral position. When you are around hostile, defensive people there is a natural tendency to become cautious and a little defensive yourself.)

After listening for over half of the session to their shouts, tears, and exchanges of accusations, each one protecting himself from the other, I asked if they had any idea how the other one was feeling.

Between her tears and sobs the wife replied, "He doesn't have any feelings."

"What do you know about feelings?" he shot back. "All

you are interested in is what I do or don't do to please you."

Then I asked, "Are you trying to tell us that you do have some feelings you aren't talking about?"

After a brief hesitation, he replied, "Yes."

There was something different in that reply. He had said that one little three-letter word in a tone of voice I had not heard from him before. It came out quietly and honestly.

Now the office was so quiet we could hear each other breathing. Another unusual thing was happening: he had his wife's undivided attention, something he had been trying for unsuccessfully since the session began. Gently I asked him why he had not talked about his feelings before.

After more silence, two more words slipped from his lips, "I'm afraid."

Like an echo came a reply from the other voice in the room, "Me, too."

Two individuals who had previously conducted simultaneous filibusters to protect themselves from the verbal attack of the other now sat speechless. They silently looked at each other as frightened strangers in new territory. I knew, and so did they, that they were being open and honest with their feelings for the first time in who knows how long. They knew now what it was to be real. Intimacy had been established, and they were on their way.

This experience was also profound for me, for I became aware of how frightening it really is for some people to be open. I also noted how dramatically *my* feelings changed toward this couple as they dropped their defensiveness and revealed some of their real feelings.

This couple continued to see me in weekly sessions. In the beginning I was certain they were a "one-session couple," but what started in the first appointment was a process of growing trust in one another as well as in others. Through this growth, they began to experience a new joy in their marriage.

THE FEAR OF REJECTION

Behind all defensiveness is fear—fear of not being accepted or understood. Knowing this, I try to reach beyond defensiveness to the fear itself. You need to do this in your marriage as well. It can be done if you do not allow your intolerance of the guardedness to overtake your efforts to understand. To attack the defense is counterproductive; it heightens and reinforces protective walls. By showing understanding, the walls are no longer needed.

The *fear of rejection* or not being accepted is no doubt the most powerful of all fears. We become acquainted with it early in life, and it becomes increasingly pronounced during our adolescent years.

Think back to the time you asked that cute young girl out for a date. Remember how you experienced anxiety and agony over the possibility of her saying no? Nothing could have been worse! My wife tells me women go through this same anguish just waiting to be asked. We may laugh about it now, but the feelings were real then and the impact was great.

The other night I happened to watch a television talk show during which one of Hollywood's masculine actors was interviewed. This man's fame has come through playing roles of fearlessness in the face of danger. As he talked on the show, he revealed this trait is part of his real life as well. He said he acquired it because he is familiar with success, seldom failing at whatever he does. Being previously married and divorced, he was asked if he ever intended to marry again. To my surprise he said, "No, I failed at it once and it scares me."

Rejection is powerful, and the fear of it touches everyone, even the strongest. John Powell sums it up in the question that became the title of his book, *Why Am I Afraid to Tell You Who I Am?* "I am afraid to tell you who I am because, if I tell you who I am you may not like who I am, and it's all that I have."[2] This question and answer acknowledges that rejection is a possibility, and if it occurs you will have nowhere else to go in that relationship. Therefore, a marriage that is becoming defensive is one where there is a growing fear of rejection.

If someone is afraid of being rejected, the logical thing most people do is to work at being accepted. In early childhood, we learn that doing what others expected was a reliable source of acceptance. However, one thing was wrong. You were accepted and received approval only as long as you kept it up. From making your bed each morning to getting good grades in school, you learned what it took to form and maintain relationships.

This same basis for relationships often continues from childhood into your adult world and the marriage relationship. If your acceptance only comes from earning it, you keep doing more and more until you get tired. Weighing the need for continuing the relationship against your fatigue, you will either risk the loss of the relationship by stopping all those efforts or you will press on in a constant state of fatigue.

There is a solution. Let me point it out: "But now the righteousness of God apart from the law is revealed, being witnessed by the Law and the Prophets, even the righteousness of God which is through faith in Jesus Christ *to all and on all who believe*" [italics mine].[3]

Here God sets forth not only the plan for eternal life, but also a model for us to follow in our marriage—a model of unconditional acceptance. In following God's example of accepting us unconditionally, we are told to reach out to our marriage partners with understanding and accept them with their strengths and weaknesses—the good and the bad—just as we promised on our wedding day. Then neither we nor our partners fear, for we are accepting each other in the same fashion as we are accepted by God, who created us and loved us first.

Chapter Six

Twice They Were Strangers

"I don't even know you." The words echoed down the clinic corridor as the lady rushed out of my office in tears. She stormed down the stairs and out into the parking lot. In her outburst she was referring not to someone she had never met, but to her husband who was still sitting stunned in my office.

"I guess we *are* strangers," he muttered as he searched his pocket for the keys to his car.

Although they still lived together, they had come in separate cars—one more evidence of the estrangement that had been growing for years.

"I'll call you if anything changes," he said, as he left to follow his wife's trail to the parking lot.

As I watched out the window I saw him pause for a moment, searching the lot for her car. She had already gone. Like a person with no place to go, he slowly got into his car and drove away alone. I never heard from either of them again.

STRANGERS A SECOND TIME

At one time in the past, all married couples were strangers. Then they met and began to date. As they grew to know each other better, they began to court, became engaged, and finally married.

As I mentioned in the previous chapter, some married people never really get to know each other. They remain strangers because they share only a *part* of themselves with each other.

But far more painful to behold are husbands and wives who were close and intimate in the early years but have now grown apart to become strangers for the second time. Only those who have experienced this can know the lonely hurt of remembering the way they were—it *was* so good.

Becoming strangers in a marriage can be compared to one's dying of cancer. The separateness grows, continually snuffing out more life of the relationship, until it ends in divorce. Some have said that divorce is worse than death, because physical death is final. In the death of a marriage, the relationship keeps coming back to life, only to die again and again.

SEEKING A SUBSTITUTE FOR YOUR SPOUSE

An early sign of estrangement is a spouse's seeking to have personal needs met outside of the marriage. The couple begins to turn away from each other to new sources of support. The needs that were previously met by the marital partner are now being satisfied somewhere else. In the initial stages it can be subtle. If you have a need to spend increasing amounts of time with friends, your job, church committees, or even your children, at the expense of time with your partner, examine your motivation.

I see people turning elsewhere because it simply feels good. They satisfy their basic needs for love and a sense of worth through someone other than their marriage partner.

In group therapy I recently observed a new couple who appeared content and well-adjusted on the surface, but there was a subtle emptiness underneath.

I listened intently as they praised each other on how well they carried out the separate tasks in which each of them was heavily involved. Having been married for over twenty years, the husband related how his wife had been a model mother. She had put her children ahead of everything else.

Similarly, she praised her husband's dedication to his work, which she said consumed most of his time. His total commitment to his job had nicely moved him up the ladder of promotions and pay raises. Providing well materially for his family had helped remove any guilt.

Suddenly it hit me. Listening to them elaborate on all their responsibilities, I noticed that neither had included their marriage on the list. *They were staying busy to avoid each other!*

Furthermore, as dedicated Christians they had developed excellent "spiritual" sources for getting the personal recognition they needed. Let's face it: we all need personal recognition. The problem comes in the source of this acknowledgment. If more and more of it comes from outside the marriage, the marriage will definitely weaken.

The difficult task ahead for this couple was to give up their established substitute sources to return to their marriage for recognition and support. Both agreed they had been close at the beginning of their marriage. But back then, before children and career success came, all they had was each other.

SEEKING A SUBSTITUTE FOR YOURSELF

Another sign in this malignant process of estrangement is when one spouse *overly encourages* the other to find fulfillment outside the marriage. This happens when both seem more interested in having their own needs met than meeting the needs of their partner. By encouraging your spouse to meet more and more of his or her needs outside the marriage, the pressure is taken off you to meet them within the marriage.

At this point let me say I realize not all of your needs will be met in your marriage. This would be placing unrealistic expectations on that relationship. Nor am I saying you should not be committed to your job, your children, your church, or other important tasks outside the marriage. The problems come when these activities and the resulting relationships *replace* the marriage as the source for feeling worthwhile and loved. Even when outside sources are recognized, it is difficult to lower their priority to once again make room for the marriage.

An increasing sense of being uncomfortable when alone with your spouse also indicates a failing marriage. In response to this feeling you will find yourself becoming more involved in activities and situations that take you away from your partner. More and more of your time will be spent with others, and the time you are with your spouse will be spent jointly with other couples.

Friends are great. Every couple needs them to complement their marriage. The trouble in outside sources comes when you find that you must have others around all the time in order to feel comfortable with your mate. Intimacy is then on the way out.

THE CHALLENGE OF REBUILDING THE RELATIONSHIP

Can husbands and wives who have become strangers ever be best friends again? Is there a way to treat the failing marriage that is close to dying? Can there be an alternative to divorce or living within a sick marriage? Yes! Let me show you how.

First of all you need to *decide* you are going to rebuild the relationship rather than end it. Without this decision nothing will happen. When you make that determination to stay married and work on it, you need to know that (1) it is God's will and (2) that the process is usually slow and difficult. Some couples who have gone through it have referred to the pace as "growth by inches." At times it is so gradual they are certain nothing is happening.

You will recognize that aliveness does come back as you rebuild your lines of communication, however. Once again you will begin to see signs of life in your marriage. By life, I mean experiencing those good, warm feelings from the marriage relationship rather than from outside sources.

As your marriage comes back to life, so will you. The deterioration that has been destroying your union reverses.

The desire to give to each other once again becomes basic in the marriage.

Let me make one more point on the challenge of your rebuilding. Although counseling is helpful and even necessary for many in achieving this change, I am the first to admit that not all couples need outside help to do it. However, *everyone* working on resolving their problems, whether they are in counseling or not, will be required to face the *test of patience* while the relationship heals and begins to grow again. One consolation to remember is that it also took time for the marriage to break down in the first place.

To rebuild your marriage you must go back to the basics. Remember that all relationships, including your marriage, are formed and maintained by the desire of each person to meet the other's needs. Create a setting whereby your partner cannot help but respond to you. For instance, suppose you would like more attention from your wife in the evenings. Rather than demanding it, start doing the supper dishes, putting the children to bed, or doing any other task that routinely takes her away from you at that time. Wives, if you would like more of your husband's attention on Saturday afternoon, start cutting the grass for him or washing the family car so that this time is free for both of you. You may have better ideas, more suitable for you. But find a way to meet each other's needs in your marriage.

In answer to my question "What advice would you give to Christian couples with marital problems?" one evangelical leader, who is himself dealing with such problems, told me: "You must learn that the feelings of romance in a marriage *follow* the acts of love—doing loving things. When we begin to do the right, loving thing toward those whom we are commanded to love (whether we feel like it or not) God compensates by giving the *feelings*."

In order to meet each other's needs, you must first know what they are. This will often create an immediate risk of being vulnerable because of the possibility of rejection if your needs are ignored. Revealing your needs only to have them rejected is fertile ground for emotional hurt. Consequently, before you divulge your most intimate needs you must feel secure so that the risk is tolerable.

THE STEPS TO REBUILDING YOUR MARRIAGE

There are definite steps to rebuilding your marriage. They include *commitment, revealing needs,* and *adjustment*. As each step begins, the others keep working. When the rebuilding process is operating in full force, all three steps function like a synchronized team.

STEP ONE: COMMITMENT

Commitment means you accept your partner unconditionally and that you will always be there *no matter what*. It is the absence of rejection. Commitment is taking your hands off the doorknob to the back door of your marriage. You will find that commitment and risk-taking grow simultaneously as your marriage is tested by more and more openness. However, until your unconditional promise of commitment is established you cannot proceed in rebuilding. This must be your decision, and it must come before the other steps.

Inherent in your commitment is your willingness to let go of bad feelings and memories from your marital past. I am referring to those events that initially created distrust and caused your needs to go unmet. Regardless of whether you or your spouse were responsible for them, both of you must let go of them.

No matter how difficult it may seem to be, keeping at the rebuilding process is a growth factor in itself. Even though nothing may seem to be happening, *the commitment not to quit* reflects a belief and confidence in the future of the marriage. This commitment also implies an acceptance of the other person and the marriage as a whole.

At one time I was seeing an insecure young couple in a therapy group. Week after week they kept telling us they were not going to continue coming, and that divorce was a serious alternative to solving their problems.

However, they kept coming back.

Then one night, in distinct contrast to other evenings, they looked much better. They were relaxed and discussed with confidence some of their unsolved problems. Sensing the improvement, one of the members asked if their marriage was better.

"Not really," replied the wife. "We still have all our problems, and our communication is as lousy as ever."

The session continued and nothing more was said about it until the end, when one of the other members asked them the question that had become routine, "Will we see you next week?"

To everyone's surprise they said, "Yes, we have decided to definitely give this a try." Commitment to the group and to each other had been established. Progress followed closely. Incidentally, the group's acceptance of them also took one giant step forward.

STEP TWO: REVEALING NEEDS

Once there is evidence of commitment, risks lessen and each spouse begins to reveal more of his personal needs to the other. These needs vary from mowing the lawn and cleaning the house to sitting together under the stars, sharing innermost thoughts and feelings. Realize that *all* of your needs are important—both the practical and the emotional. Actually they are all interrelated.

Realize that your needs are unique to you. Only you know what they are; therefore, only you can adequately communicate them to your spouse. Too often we expect our partner to know our needs without our revealing them.

It is easy to hide your personal needs behind critical statements pertaining to your spouse's behavior. And usually your spouse hears only the criticism and fails to detect the need. So instead of responding to the need, he or she tends to become defensive.

Suppose you want to sit alone with your spouse in the yard after the children are in bed. The critical statement would be, "You never sit with me in the yard after we have the kids in bed." (Incidentally, the words "never" and "always" are deadly words that raise our defensiveness and are certain to start a fight or stop communication.)

Focusing more on the need than the criticism, the same message would be, "One of the nicest times of the day for me is when we can sit alone in the back yard after the kids are in bed. Even though we seldom do it, I really need that time alone with you."

Analyze how you would have responded to these two different messages. Obviously, the second statement is better. It does not criticize the partner but rather, gives that person room to respond voluntarily to the need. *Do not tell your spouse what to do; rather, state what you need.*

STEP THREE: ADJUSTMENT

If relationships are built and maintained on your meeting one another's needs, then it is not enough just to know what those needs are. You must respond to them. This is where adjustment comes in—that fundamental thread that runs through all relationships.

The strength of any relationship is centered on each partner's willingness and ability to make changes in themselves for the purpose of meeting the other person's needs. If you are flexible and sensitive to your spouse's needs, the relationship grows. On the other hand, if you are rigid and uncompromising, the relationship will wither and die.

To truly understand adjustment you must be able to differentiate between the *willingness to change* and the *ability to change*. They are often erroneously considered the same, feeding unwarranted hostility in a relationship. You may question your spouse's motivation to change if you feel he is *unwilling* to change, though in reality, he may be *unable*. If a desired change is not occurring in your marriage, determine for yourself whether your spouse is unwilling or unable to make that change. Mistaking one for the other becomes extremely frustrating for both partners.

This "willing" and "able" distinction was made clear to me by a couple I was seeing at a rural medical clinic where I consulted once a week. There was not much room in their lifestyle for feelings. Only one thing was important to them: *work!*

During one session the wife told me her husband never said, "I love you." She went on to say that she would like to have him do this, "just like the neighbor's husband tells his wife."

My logical question, of course, to the husband was, "Do you love your wife?"

I knew the challenge ahead of me when he replied, "I'm here, ain't I?"

When I asked him if he would be willing to start telling her that he loved her, he replied, "I suppose I could. But the words tend to stick in my throat. I never heard my folks say it to each other, nor did anyone tell it to me when I was growing up."

As our session continued I learned that during the winter months, part of his daily routine was to get up before his wife every morning, put on the coffee, brush the snow from her car, and start the engine. Then when she was ready to leave for work, her car was nicely warmed. She had a factory job ten miles away, which helped out financially during the slim winter months.

"Do you enjoy getting up and doing this each morning?" I asked.

"I hate it!" was his immediate reply. "The only person in the world I would do that for is sitting right there," he said, pointing at his wife.

At that very moment she and I simultaneously realized that that was his "I love you." He would have been *willing* to say the words, but he did not have the *ability* to convey it verbally as sincerely as he did with his actions.

Once your partner knows your needs there must be the freedom to meet them in his or her own unique way. Only then is it sincere and real.

Adjusting to one another's needs does not come automatically. Three important ingredients are involved, and they all must work together as a unit.

First you must *know yourself*. To be able to adjust and make effective changes you must be in touch with who you are. Get a realistic hold of your strengths and weaknesses. Clarify in your mind your likes and dislikes. Knowing yourself well is essential, for adjustment entails making changes in yourself for the benefit of your partner.

Second, you must *understand your spouse*. Try to successfully understand your partner without cluttering the understanding with your personal judgments and opinions. At this point try to remain objective. Ask what it is that is real. Put meaning behind your spouse's feelings and behavior. To the best of your ability, try to determine their cause and effect.

Once you *understand* these needs, even though you may not agree with all of them, adjustment will be easier and more effective. Realize that understanding your partner's feelings and behavior does not necessarily mean you agree.

Third, to successfully adjust to your partner you must *be skillful in communicating*. Communication is extremely powerful in the success of any relationship. Do not underestimate it! The problem most often mentioned to me by couples seeking counseling is, "We can't communicate." On the other hand those couples who improve inevitably tell me, "Now we can talk."

Chapter Seven

What to Do When the Feelings Are Gone

"Our marriage is dead!"

"We don't feel anything for each other anymore!"

"I still appreciate my spouse, but we make better roommates than lovers."

How often these statements open counseling sessions as a spouse tries to cope with a marriage in which romance seems to have vanished. "Roommate," "brother/sister," and "good friend" are all labels the partner uses in an attempt to describe with kindness and respect a disintegrating marital relationship.

Remember the words you used so easily when you first met and fell in love? How long has it been since you called your partner Sweetheart, Honey, or Darling? Do those words now tend to stick in your throat? Maybe you've forgotten how to pronounce them. Has it been that long? Why have you stopped? Do your feelings appear to be dead?

Karen brought these questions into my office after she returned from a college class reunion. She told me she was afraid of what she had felt toward an old classmate and needed to figure out what was wrong. For years she and her husband, Carl, had been growing apart.

"He's a nice guy and all that," she said kindly. "Just as long as he doesn't try to kiss me." She made a face as if she had eaten a sour pickle.

The feelings between them had dwindled for many years, and now the romance seemed to be gone. Karen believed it was middle age setting in. She had concluded that romantic feelings belonged only to newlyweds, who had not yet discovered the real world of marriage. She thought that some couples are able to hang on to these feelings longer than others, but eventually the humdrum of marital routine comes to them all. Carl was of the same opinion, though she didn't know it because the two of them were not communicating.

Circumstances were relatively stable in the marital rut they had created for themselves. Work, maintain the house and yard, try to raise teenagers, entertain a few friends, and then back to work. It was boring, but predictable. Also, the rut seemed safe—until the college reunion.

Carl had been in the middle of a busy sales campaign, trying to meet quotas for his company. As national sales manager, he felt pressured to make an important business trip on the same weekend as Karen's reunion. But Karen didn't mind when he opted out of going with her. Since they had met after graduation, he wouldn't have known anyone at the reunion. And Karen had thought she would probably have more fun and freedom without him, anyway.

Arriving at the reception a little late, she walked into a room full of people. She was quickly caught up in reminiscing with old friends.

"One of my old classmates called to me to introduce me to a friend, Ted," Karen said. "He looked vaguely familiar, and suddenly I remembered that Ted was the nerd who had practically been a recluse in the chemistry lab. He had really changed—for the better.

"I found myself being drawn to him," Karen continued. "He looked terrific! Both of us just stared at each other, aware something strange was going on between us. The silence became awkward until he finally said something. I don't remember what it was, but I remember being frightened of falling into a situation with Ted that I couldn't handle. He was also alone at the reunion, which fueled our strong feelings because of the time we could spend together."

The excitement of infatuation battled guilt and fear in Karen's mind. She knew it was wrong but loved the way she felt. The two-day reunion came to an end. Nothing had happened that either Karen or Ted regretted, but Karen had learned that her feelings were still alive. It was her marriage that seemed dead. And this was what prompted her to schedule an appointment at my office.

Karen's story is not unique. Convinced that feelings of love and passion are forever relegated to the past, couples move into middle age and beyond. Their marriage becomes dull and routine. Suddenly, through some unexpected event, old feelings are awakened in one spouse, but with someone else. Then he or she becomes depressed as the marriage seems more lifeless than ever.

THE SEARCH FOR PASSION

For many couples the search for passion gets off track early in their efforts because they are looking for the wrong thing. What Karen felt for Ted was infatuation, a primarily physical, sexual attraction with no commitment. It is a well-disguised form of lust.

At first the infatuation is appealing because it possesses all the excitement of physical attraction without the cost of commitment. This attraction is not intended to last, however, and will never continue over the years in marriage. What couples are really seeking is something much better than infatuation—passion in its truest and highest form.

Passion is a compelling emotional drive demonstrated by caring and fondness. The sexual element of marriage belongs within the context of passion. It becomes the physical confirmation for the level of intimacy that has developed between the couple.

The key to a successful beginning in your search for intimacy is to realize that passion is not the beginning. Rather, passion is the natural result of intimacy that completes the process. Many couples never get started, because they are convinced the feelings must be present first. This is wrong.

Do not let this notion block you from the search. What precedes passion?

We get a clue from the experience of a surgeon who found Amy, his true love and, eventually, his wife, in the operating room, assisting him daily with surgery. Initially, he was not at all attracted to her. She was plain and was so introverted no one really knew her. Amy would have been the last person he would have considered inviting to a romantic, candlelight dinner. So what happened to bring them together?

After working closely in critical situations, the surgeon discovered that Amy had an uncanny ability to read his every move during surgery. She seemed to know his thoughts. She knew the way he preferred to have his instruments laid out. During surgery he would find the correct instrument in his hand without his requesting it. During surgery their four hands moved as if synchronized. And those rare occasions when Amy was absent from the operating room, he felt incomplete.

One evening, after a long day at work, they had dinner together in a little Italian restaurant near the hospital. This setting let the conversation move from a professional level to a more personal one. He discovered that Amy's intuitive sense for him carried into other areas. This sensitive understanding created an attraction more powerful than he had ever experienced.

"She seemed to know me so well it was eery," he continued. "As we talked, I discovered a compelling desire to know her at this same level of intimacy."

The harmony they shared through their profession flowed into their personal life together. First, they loved their work. Then they were drawn together by the joy of a common goal. Finally, they discovered a passion that gave birth to a romantic love leading them into marriage. Although those who knew Amy only from a distance viewed her as a plain, introverted person, her husband successfully saw all aspects of her, thus discovering the most passionate woman he had ever met.

My point is not that Amy was unique, but rather that they

found the path leading to true passion, which is available to every marriage. The roots of this passion are found in intimacy, not physical attraction. Both are present in a strong marriage, but the physical, sexual attraction is the product of an emotional, spiritual intimacy. Everyone cannot be a surgeon with an operating room to fine-tune a marriage. However, the same principles that produced passion for this couple are available to others. And the resulting passion grows over the years and lasts a lifetime.

THE INTIMACY LADDER

Let us look at this process of growing in intimacy in terms of climbing an intimacy ladder. Each step carries you to a deeper level until you reach the final step—passion. Whenever you are having difficulty maintaining your present level of intimacy, return to the previous one, rebuild, and climb again. The five steps are listed in order:

5. Passion
4. Intimacy
3. Commitment
2. Understanding
1. Learning

As you climb the intimacy ladder and fully develop each step, you will discover the next step follows automatically. True listening produces understanding. Understanding draws you to a growing openness with and trust in your partner. And that trust results in commitment.

A sense of safety must be present within the relationship before you can move on to intimacy. Listening, understanding, and commitment unlock the door to intimacy. Let me illustrate how this occurs.

Several years ago I was leading a family conference at a retreat center in northern Minnesota. The retreat was an annual tradition for several farm couples, who drove all the way from North Dakota to break away from the daily duties of rural life. During each afternoon I would offer brief, one-half hour consultations to couples. This gave an opportunity for personal questions and application of the subject matter presented in the morning seminars. Hazel took advantage of one of these sessions by dragging her husband, Herman, in for an appointment.

"Jerry, you talk about needs and feelings husbands and wives should have," Hazel blurted out, setting the agenda for the session. "Well, Herman never tells me any of those sweet things."

"Is that true?" I asked Herman.

"Yep, guess so," Herman replied. His lips were tightly sealed and his arms folded like a shield in front of him, ready to do battle.

"He never even tells me he loves me," Hazel continued.

"Have you ever told Hazel you love her?" I asked.

"Once!" he replied.

"When?" I asked.

"She knows," Herman responded.

You can see from this conversation that Herman was not in a safe atmosphere. With some urging, however, he did relate the solitary time he had actually said the words "I love you."

"As we were leaving the church on our wedding day, Hazel asked me to say it. I told her I loved her. I also told her that I was not accustomed to saying those words, so she would probably not hear them much. But I told her if I ever changed my mind and stopped loving her, she would be the first to know."

With Herman's exposition we ended our session fifteen minutes early. Hazel said that helped to know that I, too, was unsuccessful in getting Herman to relate his emotional needs and feelings. But this was not the end of the story.

Each evening we concluded our day with a fireside session in the large dining room at the lodge. About 150 people gathered for a time of questions and discussion. Because of the poor acoustics in the building, we used a microphone. But the group enjoyed this session because it was less structured and more their time than mine.

Early in one of the evening meetings a woman raised her hand to question me.

"During this week," she began, "you have been talking about the importance of married couples regularly communicating their emotional needs and feelings with each other. I would be thrilled if my husband, George, would do it just once. Tell me, why don't any of these men talk about their feelings like we women do? Don't they have any?" she asked.

George slid down in his seat trying to hide his embarrassment. A few other wives snickered and made comments under their breath. As everyone redirected their attention to the front, awaiting the "expert's" answer, I stood in silence, totally blocked on what to say. Then I noticed a man, sitting near the front of the dining hall, hesitantly raise his hand. Quickly I rushed the microphone to him, hoping he would bail me out.

"I have feelings!" he said quietly. "Lots of them." His words pierced the silence, moving the group into a new level of intimacy.

He proceeded to tell about the night when, as a little boy, he was frightened by a flash of lightning and a clap of thunder that shook the entire house. He ran to his parents' room in fear, with tears flowing down his cheeks and his heart pounding. When he tried to crawl into their bed for comfort, his father awakened, turned on the light, and looked into his son's face. "Big boys don't cry," he said sternly. "Now go back to bed." It seemed as fresh in this man's mind as if it had happened yesterday.

"I don't ever remember crying again," he said, quietly handing the microphone back to me.

You could have heard a pin drop in that large hall. I was about to ask for another question when I noticed a man across the room holding up his hand. I passed the microphone to him and he said, "I ain't got much to say, except I agree with him," nodding to the man who had just spoken.

"Me, too!" impulsively replied the man next to him.

A strange thing began to happen. The microphone made

its way through the crowd, as one man after another talked about his emotional needs and feelings. Guess where the microphone finally ended? Herman!

He referred to our meeting that afternoon, so I asked him why he felt open now. Alone in the privacy of an office, with only his wife and the counselor, he had said practically nothing. Yet now he was talking about his feelings over a public address system to 150 people. Why?

His profound response: "I feel safe here. We have all been listening to each other and a lot of us fellows understand what it was like to be forced to be men while we were still boys. Besides that, we all seem to care about the other guy."

Herman had given us the three essentials necessary to create an atmosphere of safety—listening, understanding, and commitment. These essential elements create an atmosphere of safety and are the initial steps of the intimacy ladder.

Now let's go back and look individually at each step.

LISTENING

Skillful listening is an art. More will be said in the communication chapter about the techniques of a skillful listener. However, getting a couple to listen to each other is usually the first step in marriage counseling. You interrupt both spouses from simultancously talking *at* each other and reintroduce the skill of listening.

Lloyd and Shannon had trouble communicating. Neither listened; one was forever interrupting the other in the middle of a conversation.

"You are always late coming home . . . ," Shannon began.

"What time did I get here two nights ago?" Lloyd interrupted, knowing he had been on time.

"It's your attitude that bothers me," Shannon continued.

"It's not different from yours," Lloyd retorted.

Attacks and interruptions revealed they weren't listening to each other. Frustration and defensiveness resulted.

If this is a pattern in your marriage, make every effort to hold your tongue and *listen*. When your partner has finished a statement, repeat to him or her what you have heard. Determine that you've heard correctly. Then offer your position. Chances are favorable that your message will be received in the same manner.

Effective listening includes more than merely hearing what the other person says. You must actively demonstrate listening to convey a sincere interest in your partner and in what is being said.

Consistent eye contact with affirmative nodding is a classic technique of active listening. Another subtle, powerful tool to convey active listening is to offer nonverbal responses to nonverbal messages. The classic example for the counselor is to pass the tissue box when tears begin to run down the client's face. Now we all know that the client can reach the box, but we pass it as a way of saying we are in tune with the emotions as well as the content of what is being said.

Become a skillful listener and discover the openness that emerges in the patterns of communication. Refrain from the urge to interrupt, to defend, or to clarify a point. Your partner's trust will grow as he or she perceives you to be a more understanding person. Skillful, consistent listening also displays your openness to what is being said. Listening opens the door to understanding, the second step on the ladder.

UNDERSTANDING

To understand does not always mean to agree. You can be understanding without agreeing.

Kelly and Reid, a separated couple attempting to reconcile, were discussing Kelly's new sales job. Kelly explained the importance of this job to her career fulfillment. Yet her being caught up in orientation, training, and pressure to prove herself had resulted in a lack of involvement at home that had become the obstacle to her moving back with Reid.

Most of her training was going well, but when it came to computing percentages and writing contracts, she was blocked. Numbers had never been her favorite subject. Kelly's boss was understanding, saying there was no stupid question unless it was asked more than five times. But Kelly knew it would take her more than five times to learn how to complete and compute the contracts. In desperation, she called Reid at his office one morning, hoping to get some support.

To her surprise, Reid understood. He told Kelly she needed self-confidence to sell, and she wouldn't gain confidence until she crossed the numbers hurdle. He not only understood the spot she was in but invited her to come over to his office. When Kelly arrived, Reid promptly cleared the work from his desk to give full attention to her needs. He said he would stay later that evening to complete his own work. Two hours and seven tries later she had learned the percentage computation for the contracts in her new sales position.

"I felt endearment toward him for the first time in years," Kelly said warmly, "not primarily because of the assistance he gave me, but because of what it implied. He had *understood* me and successfully demonstrated his understanding."

Reid could have used this situation as an opportunity to influence her to return to her prior homemaker role. But instead, he understood, and their intimacy grew as a result.

Understanding makes acceptance come alive within the marriage. And acceptance creates a magnetism that causes the couple to desire to spend more time together. You are simply more comfortable around people who understand you. The element of understanding, blended with trust, yields commitment, the third step.

COMMITMENT

Commitment is the powerful force that removes the risk of rejection in your relationship. What causes you to hold back part of yourself from your spouse? The answer is the fear of rejection. Commitment removes this fear and clears the way for deeper intimacy.

Listening and understanding lead us to the door of commitment. But commitment requires a conscious act of your will. You choose to be committed and you must communicate your commitment. If you remain silent, you run the risk of communicating that you've chosen not to commit.

Commitment is more than a promise. It involves your

giving yourself to your partner. The totality of your giving reflects the depth of your commitment. Negotiated compromise becomes a foreign element in your relationship if you have a deep loving commitment to each other.

A relationship does not become solid until a commitment is present. How often I have counseled with single people who go in and out of the dating scene, experiencing one attraction after another. Warm expressions of caring cause them to believe that each one of these infatuations is true love. But then, some unexpected event tests the commitment, and they discover that what seemed real is actually counterfeit.

The frightening reality is that married couples can also discover that their commitments were counterfeit. Frequently, couples on their way to the divorce court have said, "I knew this marriage was wrong on our wedding day." The commitment was spoken but never truly made.

Commitment must go both ways before it is complete. A one-way commitment exists only for a season. Eventually it will wane when commitment is not given in return. Do not misunderstand this point. Commitment is not a trade-off, conditionally given like a promise. Rather, it is an *ongoing process* that links and holds two spouses together through both the good and turbulent days of their married life. This can only happen when commitment is sealed in love.

Recall the moment in your courtship when the commitment became a reality. Remember the freedom you felt knowing that the person you cared about so deeply was becoming yours in a special way. Don't fall into the trap of letting that commitment moment, or other significant times when the commitment was reaffirmed, carry the relationship.

Commitment is an ongoing process. This means that on a daily basis you keep the commitment alive by saying it in your own special way. Your expression of commitment must show your partner that you are consciously thinking of him or her. Whether it is the timely telephone call or a rose from the corner vendor, communicate your commitment often.

Then the fear of rejection will dissipate, and intimacy, which is the fourth step on the ladder, will emerge.

INTIMACY

Intimacy is having the freedom to be yourself with your partner. As you freely expose all that you are, you lose the fear of judgment and of rejection. We all desire and need intimacy. The lack of it causes a majority of couples to seek counseling. But because of previous hurts and rejections, we erect walls and defenses to protect ourselves from further emotional pain. Thus our ability to experience intimacy is blocked. Persistent loving attention given in an atmosphere of safety will be required for these walls to come down.

Don't quit when the response you desire is slow in coming. When your progress seems minimal on the outside, look within yourself for this is where God's work is being accomplished.

The quest for intimacy is further complicated by detours of the world, such as popular music and films, which lead men and women down roads of fantasized romantic bliss, all in the name of love. The truth is intimacy is earned. It is the product of all the work of listening and understanding, which develops a trust that yields commitment.

One fanciful detour is the notion that intimacy is always an emotional state. Closeness, worthy of the label intimacy, can be found in many ways. One of the most intimate experiences that draws me to another occurs when we share a new thought. Some of my closest times with Judy have been those occasions, when she gave me new insight on a passage of Scripture. The Lord has used her to be one of my main teachers and advisers.

Shared experiences can do the same. Recall in your marriage a time when your relationship was put to the test as you successfully endured an adventure. Can you reexperience the closeness that existed as you relied solely on each other?

Judy and I experience a warm closeness as we recall the midwinter trip we made home to Minnesota while we were in graduate school in Nebraska. Our little Renault had a serious leak in the radiator, which caused the car to overheat every twenty to twenty-five miles and required frequent stops to fill the radiator. We needed the car, but I was too broke to pay the huge repair bill, so my father had offered to help us trade cars if we could get it back to Minnesota.

We immediately headed home. Considering the heavy flow of liquid from the radiator, our only recourse was to fill the tank with water. We kept the engine running so the whole system wouldn't freeze. The four-hundred mile trip became even more tricky later in the evening as service stations began to close. In desperation we were consigned to approach farm houses where lights were still burning. We also had to endure the routine warning of each farmer as he watched us pour water into the radiator in freezing temperatures.

Near midnight, we still had fifty miles and two farm stops to go. Between tears and laughter from fatigue, Judy suggested we pray. In a brief, muddled prayer, she asked the Lord to heal the car. What? Yes, you heard me correctly, *heal the car*. Miraculously, for the last fifty miles the car did not overheat. Her prayer had been answered. Upon arrival at my parent's home I had to inspect the radiator. Across the infamous hole, the dripping water had frozen, forming a temporary seal on the radiator.

When Judy and I recall such experiences, we always feel the intimacy we shared during those times. Remember them often in your own marriage and reexperience that intimacy.

The freedom of intimacy based on an unconditional acceptance and reliance upon each other leads you to affection. First, you touch with your emotions, blending together your minds and hearts. Then you touch physically, leading you to passion, the top rung of the ladder.

PASSION

What comes to your mind when you think of passion? As a Norwegian, I claim a passion for *lefse*. My non-Scandinavian wife cannot possibly understand how I can be so fond of cold mashed potatoes mixed with lard and flour, rolled into a thin pastry and fried. I add plenty of butter and sugar when I roll the *lefse* to be eaten. Say what you will, I have a passion for *lefse*. Someone else has a passion for fishing, growing roses, playing classical music, or eating homemade apple pie.

In another arena we discover a spiritual passion as we sing the hymn, "Give Me a Passion for Souls, Dear Lord." I recall that passion being lived out during my college years by one of the saintly pastors at Pacific Garden Mission in Chicago. On those cold winter nights when we would visit and provide the evening gospel service at the mission, I observed him weeping with sadness as men and women were forced out into the cold streets because the fire marshal allowed only a set number to be housed overnight.

When an athletic team wins a championship game, we witness passion of another sort. With a shout of elation, people cheer, cry, hug, and embrace one another in victory. Whatever the cause, passion invokes a strong, compelling emotion, which draws those involved together in an outward demonstration of affection for one another.

Likewise, passion is that highest point of intimacy in a marriage, the place of exclusive closeness, which a spouse shares with no other person. Passion is intimacy at its fullest, resulting from commitment and understanding in the marriage.

Similar to the word *love, passion* is a word that has been dragged into bastardizing situations, frequently into the titles of pornographic films and printed materials. In this context passion carries an ugly connotation of lewd, erotic sexual behavior. To take passion and place it in sinful sexual contexts creates a deception of the highest order. It not only grossly confuses and misleads people seeking sexual fulfillment, but it keeps them from openly using passion in its proper context. I challenge you to reclaim passion and place it where it truly belongs—at the highest level of marital intimacy.

The passion within marriage carries all the emotional excitement experienced in other contexts and more. But marital passion possesses one ingredient which makes it unique from all other passions—the sexual element. Here the selfless giving of agape love and the fullness of the sexual experience come together. Each form of love fully develops and uplifts the other. Separate the sexual experience from agape love within the context of marriage, and passion becomes something else.

Many will argue that the sexual union can be experienced in many contexts. In one respect this is true. We have observed a change toward a more permissive society over the past decade. But the passion we are discussing here can only be found in marriage. Every other relationship is relegated second place to your spouse. A lifetime commitment to your sexual partner is a necessary requirement of marital passion.

This absolute is clearly stated in the Holy Scriptures. Look at the often quoted passage from Genesis: "Therefore a man shall leave his father and mother and be joined to his wife, and they shall become one flesh."[1]

Now consider three parts of that passage carefully: the verbs *leave* and *cleave* and the noun *one flesh*.

LEAVE

To leave mother and father, your closest familial relationships prior to marriage, makes everything else in your life second to your spouse. All of our lives are filled with relational demands, including our children. But in marriage your spouse is your primary commitment. When you fulfill this commitment, conflict does not exist in your service to each other.

CLEAVE

Only after you leave can you truly cleave. The Greek translation, *proskallao,* means "to be glued to." The cleaving in marriage is a permanent bond, never intended to be separated.[2] Properly glued, the bond becomes the strongest part of the new union. Cleaving implies an unsurpassed closeness. To cleave, you must be spiritually, emotionally, and physically close to your spouse.

ONE FLESH

You become one flesh after you cleave. The leaving *you* do, the cleaving *you* do, but the "one flesh" is a gift from God, which occurs only in the bonds of marriage. One flesh does not exist before marriage; it exists only in marriage. One flesh means that you will love your spouse exclusively, unconditionally, for a lifetime. In marriage the sexual experience finds its true home and is the only place God intended it to be experienced.

A sexual relationship outside of marriage is sin. It is based on a lustful self-centeredness, which puts self ahead of godly obedience and reflects a disregard for your partner. You may argue that your extra-marital relationship is "different." I predict that even though the relationship gives the outward appearance of caring and romance, its true nature will eventually surface in pain and disillusionment.

The apostle Paul compares the state of being one flesh in marriage to the love relationship between Christ and the Church, God's love for us through Christ His Son.[3] Placing marriage in this realm relegates it above human understanding into the realm of the holiest of relationships. This is marriage as God intended it to be.

Climb the intimacy ladder and claim the experience of godly passion: "And they were both naked . . . and not ashamed."[4]

Chapter Eight

Communication: The Food That Feeds Your Marriage

I stepped into the waiting area to invite Dan and Debby into my office for their session. I noticed they were sitting in opposite corners hiding behind their magazines. Totally ignoring each other, they marched into my office. *It is going to be like pulling teeth to get this couple to talk today,* I thought. I closed the door and took my place, clipboard in hand to make notes during the session. The silence was heavy.

"How was your week?" I asked trying to get something started.

"I've got nothing to say," Dan replied. He looked ready to explode.

I glanced at Debby who immediately disintegrated into tears. "He just doesn't understand," she blurted between sobs. Grabbing a tissue from the table, she blew her nose, and the silence returned.

"We love each other," Dan jumped in. "We just can't talk."

"Don't you speak at all?" I inquired.

"Oh we talk," replied Debby, "but we don't *really* talk."

What does it mean to "really talk"? Have you ever felt tension in a relationship? Or like this couple, has it happened within your marriage? Then you have a *good talk* and everything seems better. Reflect for a moment on your conversation. Quite often nothing new or significant was said, but the conversation helped the relationship. Why?

THE VALUE OF COMMUNICATION

The answer lies in an important principle which one must understand to appreciate fully the value of communication. *The experience of communicating is as important to the well-being of the relationship as the subject matter being communicated.* Communication is the food that feeds a relationship and nourishes a marriage.

Dan and Debby needed this experience. During our session I decided I would not only help them learn communication skills but also provide a way for them to experience the process of healthy communication.

More than 75 percent of all couples who seek marital counseling discover that a lack of communication skills is a significant contributor to their problem. If a couple cannot communicate effectively with each other, all the principles, attitudes, and goals available to improve their marriage will fall short of success. Nothing of significance will transpire until healthy lines of communication exist.

Communication is the vehicle that moves you from one level of the intimacy ladder to the next. You need to fully understand the importance of communication and sharpen your communication skills.

Dan was trying to relate to Debby but was having difficulty. "I really don't know what you mean by communication," he commented.

"I can't put it into words," Debby replied. Turning to me, she asked, "Can you help?"

"Let me try," I said, walking to a chalkboard in my office. I wrote the following for them: "Communication is the *skillful ability* to both *accurately and successfully* express one's *thoughts, feelings,* and *expectations* to one's partner and the *ability to perceive* what is being said in return."

Dan frowned. "That's too academic for me. I feel like I'm back in school."

"Let me try to make this more personal for you," I replied.

They seemed intently interested in learning, so for the first part of the session I became an instructor.

SKILLFUL ABILITY

Communication requires skill. Therefore, it is something you learn. If you are a good communicator, reflect on how you learned the skills. If you are not a good communicator, you can learn. I showed Dan and Debby that neither of them had experienced good communication role models from their parents. However, they could learn now by acquiring the skills and practicing them.

ACCURACY AND SUCCESS

Their message needed to be accurate. Say what you mean. Some common pitfalls can result from inaccurate communication. A message can be accurate but still not be successfully understood by the other person. If this is your case, you are still not communicating.

Several years ago when I served on a hospital staff, I made grand rounds with the interns and residents in our teaching program. Because of my nonmedical background, they could easily lose me during their technical discussions. Their communication was extremely accurate, but meant nothing to me. With me, their communication was not successful. Be sensitive to the person with whom you are communicating, and adapt your message so they can understand.

THOUGHTS, FEELINGS, AND EXPECTATIONS

Consider, too, the content of what is being communicated. Thoughts are usually the easiest to convey with the least amount of risk. Feelings are more difficult to express, depending on what the feelings are. Expectations deserve special comment with respect to the marriage relationship.

When I mentioned expectations, Debby spoke up. "If I have to ask for a favor from my husband, it doesn't really count."

Dan now got back into the conversation, responding, "Why can't you help me out a little by telling me what you need or expect?" He grinned and said, "I'm a slow learner, but I do learn."

"O.K., I'll try." The couple was beginning to communicate.

TWO-WAY COMMUNICATION

Communication is always a two-way process. Not only is a message sent, but it must be heard and understood, and may require a response. Here the communication circle is completed. Skillful communicators understand the importance of this two-way process and become sensitive to their need to respond to the messages they receive. Dan and Debby agreed that from then on they would try to respond in some way, indicating that they had heard their spouse's message.

"Can you teach us some of the best ways to communicate?" Dan asked.

Returning to the chalkboard, I listed some of the most common ways.

TOOLS OF COMMUNICATION

Methods of Sending	*Methods of Receiving*
1. Words	1. Hear
2. Expressions	2. See
3. Deeds	3. Feel
4. Actions	
5. Gestures	
6. Touch	
7. Silence	

In the sending and receiving of messages a variety of tools are available to us. The above list shows some of the more frequently used methods.

"There are many ways to say the same thing," I told the couple.

"That's for sure," Debby said, looking directly at her husband. "Teach him how to use words to tell me he loves me. He is great at fixing anything that breaks in the house. He says that's the way he expresses his love to me, but somehow repairing the leaking faucet just isn't the same as speaking words."

"Skillful communicators are able to combine the various methods in a way that best says what they think and feel," I responded. "Realize that communication is far more than words. Gestures, actions, deeds, and expressions can be powerful tools of communication." Dan smiled, feeling I had taken his side on that one.

I went on to explain that silence can also make a strong statement. This tool brings to light the important principle of timing. A good communicator not only knows what to say but *when to say it*. Silence can strongly underscore a nonverbal message of caring and commitment. Become skillful at determining when to speak words and when to let silence make the statement.

When communication breaks down, the problem usually lies not in talking, but in poor listening skills. Dan claimed that Debby frequently interrupted him before he finished what he was saying.

The list of receiving (listening) skills is short, but equally important. Listening begins with hearing—hearing the words, the tone of voice, the sighs and the groans. One woman in a couples therapy group said her husband always became frustrated when she talked about problems. The group challenged her, stating that he seldom said a word. "But listen to him breathe," she replied, mimicking a heavy sigh, which routinely came from him during these times.

A sensitive listener also learns the importance of listening with the eyes. Pick up all the nonverbal messages from body language and facial expressions. Learn to perceive the nonverbal messages, and you will not only better understand what is being said but you will convey interest in the other person. Remember the role that listening plays in creating an atmosphere of safety. After Dan and Debby had each voiced their struggles, each felt heard and understood. My office had become a safe place for them to talk.

A third means of listening is by using your intuition, your feelings. Examine what you are feeling as someone communicates with you. This, too, is part of the message and has meaning. Consider the emotions you experience, such as warmth, anger, happiness, tension, as you communicate.

Remember, the feelings experienced during communication are part of the total message.

A few years ago I discovered how the feeling aspect of listening helped me detect a change in the message. As a family, we had taken a day to visit one of the vacation developments that sold real estate at inflated prices. As a marketing technique, we were promised either a camera, pots and pans, or a new car, just for taking a sales tour.

When we arrived, I made it clear to the salesperson that we did not intend to buy property. As we took the required tour, the friendly salesperson complimented me on my family while making an excellent presentation of the property.

Before we completed our tour he said, "I'm sure after seeing this fine vacation site you want to reconsider this opportunity for your family. You seem to be a person who would know a good business deal when he saw one." He expressed concern for my family's well-being and complimented me on my business savvy. The gentleman's words *seemed* sincere. But my *feelings* told me otherwise.

Similar experiences have probably happened to you. Whether it was a sales situation or a confusing message from your spouse, listen to your feelings along with the words and find the complete meaning. Incidentally, we did not buy a lot, but we did get our camera.

"If you get frustrated while communicating a message, there is a good chance you are not being heard," I told Dan and Debby. "What can be even more confusing are those times when the spouse *seems* to be listening but isn't."

"Now you're hitting close to home!" Debby exclaimed. Dan knew she was referring to those all too frequent times when he became preoccupied.

We refer to this preoccupation as *selective inattention*. The listener selectively chooses not to receive a message while giving the appearance of listening.

Avoidance is the most common form of selective inattention. The listener appears to be accepting the message, but there is a subtle, or sometimes not so subtle, shift in the focus. Watch for those unexpected changes in subject in the midst of a conversation. Avoidance may be at work.

Another method of selective inattention is to *placate*. A person placates with overly complimentary references that block the true message. This technique of appeasement becomes an unspoken message of *Don't bother me with your problem. I don't want to hear about it.*

"This reminds me of when you took over the finances after that fierce money argument several months ago," Dan said to his wife.

"When I was having trouble making all the payments, I asked for my husband's assistance," Debby told me. "Do you remember your response?" she asked her husband.

"Sure," he said. "I told you, 'You are the best money manager. I know you can find a solution to our shortage of funds.'"

"That's right," Debby retorted, "and according to what we are learning today, that is placating."

I explained how a compliment and verbal reassurance in such a context is an unspoken rejection that says, "That's your problem. You wanted it, now you can have it."

"What should we do if this continues to happen?" Debby asked.

"As a general rule, resolution comes when a couple refocuses from the content of their conversation to the manner in which they are communicating," I answered.

A refocusing statement could be, "I don't feel that I am being heard." Another approach would be to have the listener repeat in his or her own words what was understood. This is called *active listening*.

When strong emotions or confusion continue to block constructive communication, consider seeing a professional marriage counselor. You will be amazed at the help a third party with professional training in communication and relationships can offer you. At my suggestion, Dan and Debby decided to join a couples therapy group to continue practicing their communication skills.

FIVE SYNDROMES OF COMMUNICATION BREAKDOWN

I am frequently asked to name the most common areas of communication breakdown. The following five syndromes keep reappearing. Look for them in your relationships to keep your communication healthy and free from disruption.

1. THE DOUBLE MESSAGE SYNDROME

Sometimes, two messages are sent at the same time, one verbal and the other nonverbal. One is usually positive, the other negative. Both messages are clearly received but confusion results because the two messages conflict.

One man told me he loved my seminar sessions and could hardly wait for the week to pass so he could attend the next. Yet he consistently came late and left early. He may have had a good reason, but, until he explained, he had given a double message that required clarification.

Under these circumstances, confront the person and ask the meaning of each message. This may be difficult, but it is more productive than allowing the confusion to continue.

2. THE FALSE ASSUMPTION SYNDROME

You know what you mean when you speak or act in a certain manner. So when someone else acts or communicates the same way, you run the risk of falsely assuming this carries the same meaning and message as yours. This is not always the case.

A man in one of my couples groups said his wife always tuned him out when he spoke about any serious matter during the session. She immediately denied the accusation. When I asked him why he felt that way, the husband demonstrated his wife's nonverbal behavior by closing his eyes and holding his head with his hand, "When I become bored and turned off by a message, that is just what I do," he said.

At this point his wife clarified the meaning of her behavior. She said, "My husband often accuses me of misunderstanding him. My actions reflect my intense concentration on his message." She had determined to make every effort during group therapy sessions to hear him clearly. The group felt she was sincere and helped her husband see that the same behavior in both of them carried opposite meanings.

Do not falsely assume a message. The person sending it is the authority on its true meaning.

3. THE FALSE PREDICTION SYNDROME

Have you ever needed to say, "Let me finish! Hear me out before you arrive at your conclusion." These pleadings alert us to the possibility of a false prediction.

A false prediction occurs when you place a meaning on what is said before the speaker has finished saying it. All too often, when the entire message is relayed, the meaning changes. Don't falsely predict, but wait and hear out your partner.

I grew up in the era of Cushman motor scooters. Several of us owned them, and it became a weekly routine to patrol the block around the village park on Wednesday evenings during the local band concert. Part of the fun was to offer cute girls a ride around town. Those of us with scooters had the obvious edge over the other guys.

My scooter was wearing out. I had purchased it used, and it was in need of constant repair. One particular time I needed a new drive chain. My old one had become so worn that it constantly jumped the sprocket, especially when I rode double.

Having saved money for a new chain, I asked my father if he would purchase the replacement when he made an emergency trip to the next town to pick up some items for his hardware business. I pleaded that it would not take much time. Besides, it was Wednesday, the night to patrol the park.

He listened but warned that he couldn't promise he would get it. "Only if I have time," were his words as he left.

I went to my friend's farm that afternoon to help bale hay. At 4:00 P.M. we went into the house for a break, and I called the hardware store.

When Dad answered the telephone, I got right to the point. "Did you get the chain?" I asked with a sense of urgency.

"No, I didn't," he replied. He started to say something else, but I cut him off.

"Thanks a lot!" I said curtly as I slammed down the receiver. I sat in silence that evening during supper, picking at my food. I was so angry and disappointed that I could not even look at my father. Finally he broke the silence.

"You hung up on me," he stated, opening the conversation.

"That's right," I replied.

"I had more to say."

"I had heard enough." I knew the excuses—the customer must come first. However, Dad's next statement stopped me dead in my tracks.

"I did get to the Cushman shop," he continued. "They have a new scooter on the showroom floor that caught my eye." I wanted to crawl under the table with embarrassment but excitement overruled. Dad had my full, undivided attention.

"They are interested in taking your scooter on a trade. I put a small deposit on it until I could talk with you. I spent so much time there I need to return tomorrow to finish my errands. If you would like, we can take your scooter to make the trade."

The next day I acquired a shiny new Cushman motor scooter and learned the lesson of not predicting the meaning of a message that was partially communicated. Hear it out!

4. THE LOGIC VERSUS FEELINGS SYNDROME

When people talk and listen in the framework of *logic,* a connection is made and communication is successful. Likewise, when people talk and listen to *feelings,* successful communication occurs. However, when one person relates in the realm of logic and the other in the realm of feelings, they will pass each other without understanding. This syndrome often creates added frustration because both messages are correct, they just do not connect.

This was the problem that brought Gerald and Jennifer in for therapy. Gerald, an engineer, came from a world of logic. Jennifer, on the other hand, related everything to feelings.

They were not communicating so I placed them in a couples therapy group, hoping they would acquire new insight and skill.

After several unproductive sessions, I began to question if this was the right choice. Gerald continued to offer cause and effect solutions to every situation, missing the emotional factor. Jennifer, on the other hand, was more involved in the feelings of every situation.

One evening we had a breakthrough. In the midst of the session the following conversation transpired.

"Gerald, I think I understand what you're trying to say," commented Jennifer.

"Hold it," replied Gerald. "Did I hear you correctly? Did you say *understand?*" With a smile on his face, he declared that his wife could think after all. "This makes me feel just great," he exclaimed.

Jennifer didn't miss a beat with his dry humor. "Say it again, Gerald. Say it slowly so I can savor the sound of the word that so rarely comes from your lips."

"What word?" he asked with a puzzled look on his face.

"Feelings!" she retaliated, declaring that her husband could feel.

Although their humor entertained the group, everyone sensed a serious step had occurred as Gerald and Jennifer began to recognize each other's world of perception. They left arm in arm, reflective of their progress.

One week later everyone wanted a progress report. "How did your week go?" asked one of the group members.

"Just fine," replied Jennifer.

"For the first fifteen minutes," added Gerald.

After a brief debate over who should tell the story, they related the following.

Leaving the clinic after the last week's group therapy session, Jennifer suggested they take the romantic route home around the chain of lakes, instead of the usual freeway. There was a warm misty rain in the summer air. Jennifer snuggled next to Gerald in the car. As they neared the second lake, she suggested they park the car and walk around the lake. She told Gerald how she enjoyed the beautiful view of the skyline from that vantage point.

"I don't have time to walk," Gerald had replied. "I need to get home to prepare a report for an early morning meeting at the office. But I'll drive you around, if you like."

Jennifer tried again. "Let's get out and walk in the rain. It would be so romantic and exhilarating to feel the warm, gentle rain drops on our skin."

"I don't think we should get wet. You just had your hair done this afternoon. That would be thirty dollars down the drain. Besides, I don't want to get my new leather shoes water-stained. Why don't you roll down the window and hold your arm in the rain while I drive you around the lake?" Gerald queried in all sincerity.

Everyone in the group chuckled. The sad part was that Gerald did not understand why Jennifer was so upset. He claimed to have created a perfect solution. Jennifer could have enjoyed the mist on her skin while viewing the city's skyline. In turn, he would have arrived home at a reasonable hour—dry.

When your communication breaks down, determine if the logic/feeling pattern is interfering. You must move into one area or the other so you are communicating in the same way. My professional experience has indicated that whenever possible, it is advantageous to move from logic to feelings. Once the feelings have been heard and understood, the way is clear to look at the logical parts of the message.

If Gerald could have related to Jennifer's romantic feelings instead of offering solutions, the communication breakdown may have been prevented.

5. THE OBSTACLE OF RIGHT AND WRONG

There is definitely a place to make judgments about right and wrong on various subjects. The obedient walk of discipleship requires that you discern right and wrong behaviors and attitudes.

However, when you quickly label your spouse's response

to your message as wrong while you are "right," an immediate block in communication is created. Your partner will be inclined either to argue or withdraw. Why does this happen? By placing labels on what is being communicated, you not only reject the message, but you also imply a rejection of your partner.

Stating "I'm right—you're wrong," or using the terms *always* and *never* immediately blocks communication and leads to arguments. With each statement, you attempt to claim power and control over the other person.

Stay away from absolutes as you interact on sensitive issues. In so doing, you demonstrate respect and acceptance of the other person. In turn, it is highly probable that your mate will communicate the same acceptance and respect to you. This brings us again to listening with understanding, the key to making your marriage a safe place to communicate.

Before leaving this chapter on communication, I invite you to consider your personal prayer life. Prayer is communication with God through Christ our Lord. In James 5:16 we read: "The effective, fervent prayer of a righteous man avails much." Do you include prayer as an integral part of your marital communication?

Pray with your spouse regularly. Initially, it may seem awkward, but do it anyway. A sense of love and care will enter your marriage as you communicate together with the Source of all love.

Chapter Nine

From Saturday Night Mistress to Sunday Morning Saint

A midsummer night's dream is a rare occurrence almost anywhere, but especially in Minnesota. A night in June several years ago was one of those times. It was an ideal night, one that is indeed a dream six months later as we watch the snow swirling in sub-zero winds over the still, frozen ground.

But it was June, not December, and the setting was idyllic. The moon was full, softly lighting the patio and yard, yet casting shadows and creating forms that added mystery to the evening. There was a warm southerly breeze, the usual Minnesota chill totally absent from it. Best of all, there were no mosquitoes.

It had been the usual busy Saturday, filled with errands and chores. Now the children, who were still very young, were bathed and in bed, ready for Sunday school and church the next morning. Even though my wife and I had said nothing to each other, our minds were running on the same track. Showered and in my pajamas, I started for the bedroom when Judy said, "Go on downstairs; I'll meet you on the patio in a few minutes." I spun around and disappeared out the patio doors.

Strategically arranging two chairs in just the right places by the patio table, I sat down and waited to see what would happen next. Suddenly I seemed to forget I had been married for eighteen years and was the father of three children who were asleep inside. Rather, I had the feeling I was on a rendezvous with my mistress. I slid down in my chair, gazing off into the sky, trying to absorb and feel all that was happening around me. The words of Psalm 8 came to my mind as I looked up at the stars: "When I consider Your heavens, the work of Your fingers, / The moon and the stars, which You have ordained. . . . / O Lord, our Lord, How excellent is Your name in all the earth!"[1]

The silence was interrupted by the patio doors opening and closing. Looking up, I saw Judy standing in the moonlight with her sheer negligee flowing in the evening breeze. She was holding a tray of cheeses and fruits that were delivered before me with a warm kiss and a gentle "I love you." Although the tray of hors d'oeuvres was a labor of love, I found myself initially ignoring them, for I was captivated by this woman standing before me. I could not take my eyes off her as I found myself magnetized by her beauty. She let her body talk to me as I reached out to touch her to be sure she was real.

Responding to my gentle tug, she sat down beside me. Together we started feeding each other fruit, pieces of cheese, and kisses. We ate, talked, and touched as time seemed to stand still. There is always something exhilarating about being together outside. My eyes continued to drink in her beauty as the moonlight danced on her soft tanned skin. Even the breeze cooperated by momentarily exposing hidden parts of her body, only to cover them again. That night was one of those special nights God gives us from time to time to experience the deep love we have for each other.

As our evening together continued our feelings for each other heightened. We were both deeply aware of how much in love we were. I never dreamed I could love anyone as much as I loved her at that moment. The moon passed behind a cloud, and like an orchestra moving into the next movement of the symphony, Judy suggested we go up to bed. With my arm around her, I left that enchanted place, thanking God for this woman He had given to be my wife and for all the love we experienced together. I was deeply in love with my "Saturday night mistress," but best of all, she was also my wife.

I was awakened by the sun hitting me in the face and a voice from the kitchen yelling, "Get up, we're already ten minutes late." Stumbling out of bed, my mind still sleeping, I realized vaguely that it was morning—not just any morning, but Sunday morning. My trip to the bathroom and on to the kitchen for breakfast was interrupted by the verbal reminder to shine my sons' shoes. I arrived at the breakfast table after everyone was nearly finished.

Part of the challenge of Sunday morning breakfast is to consume it in record time without suffering from indigestion during Sunday school. My wife kept issuing the orders as the rest of us responded as a somewhat unsynchronized team, colliding as we gathered up Bibles, offering money, and a hairbrush.

As I backed out of the driveway, Judy reminded me that we had forgotten our son's Sunday school workbook. Realizing that I would not win the debate as to whether or not he really needed it that day, I pulled back in and rushed in the house to get it.

Now we were fifteen minutes late. Thankfully, Sunday morning is one time when few cars are on the freeway, so I made record driving time to church.

With my wife's direction we got into our respective Sunday school classes, out of breath but on time. My mind still racing from the short but hectic morning, I found it difficult to concentrate on the lesson. Judy's pinches on my leg, coupled with her subtle pointing to the correct verse when it was my turn to read, kept me on track and concealed quite well my preoccupation with other thoughts. Without a doubt, she was in control.

The hour passed and class was over. We started the next race—talking to everyone in the hallway long enough to be courteous while getting the kids to the restrooms and then upstairs to the sanctuary before the choir marched in. (We make it about half of the time. The other times we slip in the side door after the invocation.)

As we settled in for the morning worship service, Judy quietly leaned over to whisper that the pastor wanted to see me sometime. I wondered for a moment why he had not said something directly to me after Sunday school since we were in the same class, but I thought nothing more of it. I tried to concentrate on the sermon, but for some reason I was as restless as my two sons sitting on either side of me. Several times my wife had to remind all three of us to sit still. Part of my "problem," of course, was that I was still reliving the night before.

Judy continued to do her best to keep me in the service by finding the correct page for the hymns, opening the Bible to the Scripture passage being read, and commenting to me throughout the sermon, "Wasn't that a good point the pastor just made?" When it comes to entering into the worship service, compared to the rest of the family she indeed appeared to be the "saint."

Following the benediction we once again started our trek through the crowds to make our way to the car. As usual, we all got separated talking to different individuals. (Incidentally, the warmth and fellowship that comes from talking to various people in our church family following the service is one of the highlights of the morning for me. I wish there were some way open fellowship could be developed more into our regular services.)

Twenty minutes after the closing note on the organ, I finally made it to the car only to see that everyone else in the family had arrived ahead of me. Judy was sitting in the front seat, her door open while she visited with the pastor and his wife, who were standing next to the car.

This is when I really blew it.

Concerned that I had kept everyone else in the family waiting, and totally forgetting that the pastor had wanted to talk to me, I courteously but briefly greeted him as I got into the car, started the engine and said, "Let's be going!" I quickly pulled away from the church and started home. Tense from the hurry of the past few hours, as well as the fact that the children were tired and hungry, I drove home in a somewhat detached state of mind.

What I did not realize was that my wife was also quiet. That is unusual for her after a Sunday morning at church. As we were heading down the freeway, she broke the silence by commenting that I had certainly been cool and aloof to the pastor; furthermore, it had embarrassed her. That is when I remembered he had wanted to talk to me. I quickly rationalized that he could have said something. Her retort was that I had not given him a chance. We were starting to fight.

I looked over at Judy and observed her silent disapproval of my behavior. Listening to my feelings at that moment, I thought, "I do not even like her." I later learned she had the same dislike for me at the time. She was tense, rigid, controlling, trying to be sure we all did what was right when we were around church. Her motives were right and her intentions good, but I didn't like the way she was doing it, and I reacted extremely negatively toward her actions.

Both of us sat silently for a moment, not sure where the conversation was heading. Then it hit me.

"I don't believe it!" I said.

"Believe what?" she replied.

"How totally opposite my feelings for one person can be in less than twelve hours," I answered.

She knew exactly what I was talking about. Together, we began to notice how our responses sometimes vary so dramatically with each other's behavior. Last night I told her she was my "Saturday night mistress." She filled me with love and emotion and I fell off to sleep thanking God for her and her love. Today she became a "Sunday morning saint," once again trying to do what was best and right for everyone. But I found I wanted to avoid and ignore this person.

Which one really is the godly woman? I asked myself. I was thanking God for one and evading the other.

We learned several things from this experience. First of

all, we realized in our own marriage how important it is to openly talk out the reactions we have to each other's behavior. Our Sunday afternoon was saved because we were able to talk about the morning on the way home. How important it is to be able to deal with your feelings and talk to your partner about them as soon as you become aware of them.

The other lesson for us—and for all marriage relationships—is that when one of the partners becomes more rigid and controlling, it often has a negative effect upon the other. Although a disciplined control is good at times in our lives, expressing this between partners in a marriage usually has a negative effect. As some of my couples have said during therapy, "No one wants to be married to a critical parent."

What my wife was trying to do that Sunday morning was indeed good. What she was doing was for my benefit and for the sake of favorable appearance to others. This is why it can become doubly confusing—one spouse is trying to do what is best for the other and it is not appreciated. Our experience has helped us not to feel so responsible for one another's behavior. In other words, if I do not know which verse to read when it is my turn in the Sunday school class, it is my problem, not hers.

By the way, now that she is not keeping track for me, I have to pay closer attention myself. This rigid control of one spouse by the other is more common in evangelical marriages than in others. If you find that you dread your Sunday mornings or any other times, examine your marriage relationship. Maybe one of you is trying more than you should to run the other spouse.

There is an epilogue to this twenty-four-hour saga, by the way. Monday morning I was back at the clinic. After finishing my second appointment, my secretary informed me that the next appointment just canceled. Having a free hour and an office only five minutes away, I took the opportunity to sneak home for a surprise midmorning coffee break. The timing was perfect.

As I came in the back door Judy was just stepping out of the shower. Greeting me at the bedroom door, soaking wet, she threw her arms around me and whispered in my ear, "Your mistress is back."

I never did try to explain to my staff why I was wearing a different suit when I returned to work that morning.

Chapter Ten

The Double Bind

Ambivalence is defined as a situation in which you are experiencing conflicting pulls. Some call it being placed in a double bind.

Millions of Americans today, especially evangelical Christians, are frustrated. They realize they are being pulled in two or more directions. Responding to one pull causes a person to become more distant to the other. This is one of the most common causes for stress as people face the daily task of deciding which way to go.

Marriage is directly affected by this phenomenon and is usually one of the "pulls" in that conflict. A variety of forces can pull at the marriage. When you sort them out, however, they all seem to fall under two main categories: *time* and *money*.

Spouses frequently complain, "I am sick and tired of being third or fourth on his/her list of priorities." This person is tired of time, money, or some other interest winning out over the marriage.

"How can all this good be bad?" asked a frustrated but diligent Christian businessman. He presented convincing arguments why he should continue in each of his responsibilities. Yes, he convinced me that they all were good in themselves, but each one took him away from his wife. He was beginning to see that what initially appeared to be *good* was, in reality, *bad*.

THE TIME CONFLICT

Today we are living in a time-drained society. Everyone is busy, never having enough time to do the things they really want to do. For evangelical Christians this presents special problems. Involvement in a church schedule costs them a major portion of their nonworking time each week. On the other hand, if they do not keep up with this schedule they often experience guilt and a sense of not doing what is expected.

The "faithful evangelical church member" spends an enormous amount of time each week at church. Each Sunday, the average church member spends four and a half to five hours in church, assuming he attends Sunday school and both the morning and evening services. Of course, preparation time at home, plus commuting, is extra. And any church committee meetings scheduled before or after the services add to the time. The result is that a major portion of your "day of rest" is actively spent in the church program, often away from your family.

But the demand of time does not end on Sunday. Everyone is also expected to attend the midweek prayer service, which in the eyes of many pastors is used as a barometer to measure the members' "spirituality."

In addition to regular weekly services are the one or two evenings a week for those programs that desperately need you: choir practice, youth meetings, women's guild, men's brotherhood, and other church committees. You also may meet a couple of times a month for early morning breakfast meetings. What a great day it will be when the Christian church returns to the New Testament concept of *caring* for its people (thankfully, there are some who do), instead of putting excessive demands on them in order to sustain a program.

I challenge you to make a list of the church services and activities you are *expected* to attend each week. Next to the activity, place the estimated amount of time required and total the hours. Then, superimpose this schedule onto your work schedule and the hours required each week in your job. Add the hours in the twenty-four-hour day given to sleep. Now, how much time is left for your family? After that, determine how much time is left for just your marriage? You can now begin to understand the *double bind* you are in when it comes to time.

Over an extended period this kind of schedule has some interesting psychological effects. You become accustomed to being tired, and with the tiredness, varying degrees of hostility and frustration set in. You are careful not to let these emotions show, especially around church.

In time, you recognize your tiredness and frustration as evidences of your involvement in all these "necessary" church activities. You consider having no time for yourself, your marriage, or your family as proof of your sacrificial commitment to the program. What happens is that you become comfortable only when you are uncomfortable (tired and frustrated).

Once in a while, through no choice of his or her own, some faithful Christian who has been in this time trap for years comes out of it. Through an unlikely turn of events he finds himself off all committees. Consequently, he is not busy and becomes rested, feeling exceptionally good both physically and emotionally because he has time for himself. But can he enjoy it? No! A new twist keeps him from the joy and happiness the Lord has provided for him.

When you are exhausted, frustrated, and even depressed for a long time, you find it a real problem to once again enjoy feeling good, even though you are rested and have some time for yourself and your marriage. These good feelings are new and therefore strange to you. New feelings are difficult to accept, even when they are better than the old ones.

Rather than just accept and enjoy the good feelings, many Christians encounter a new problem. Because of their previous conditioning, they believe feeling rested implies they are not busy, thus they are not good workers. This introduces guilt. The guilty person says, "I feel rested and have time; therefore I must not be carrying my share of the load."

This is exactly the psychological double bind where many Christians find themselves. Are you one of them? Are you either rested and guilty or busy and tired? Either way you lose! You are in a trap whereby you cannot truly feel *good*.

This double bind was never God's plan for your Christian life or for your marriage. I am convinced that being caught in this losing predicament is a major weapon Satan uses to shoot down the joyful Christian and destroy the Christian marriage.

Evangelical churches today are filled with husbands and wives in this condition. Not only do they not know how to get out of it, but they don't even know they are in it! It can be a deception of the first order. I know people who do not feel good about all the good they are trying to do. It's chaos! Take a close look at what is happening not only to you but also to your relationships—especially your marriage.

THE MONEY CONFLICT

As I mentioned earlier, money is the other force that has a major control on our lives. This is partly true because of the time required to earn it. But it goes further.

Following a group therapy session I co-led with a psychiatrist friend, I learned an important lesson about money. We were desperately trying to figure out the significance of one group member's behavior. Each week he would go on and on about how frustrated he was living with a roommate he could not tolerate. Yet to the group's dismay, he would never do anything to change his situation, and he became angry whenever anyone suggested he move out.

Finally, one bit of significant information was revealed to us. This person was paying a token rent to the other person who owned the house and apparently didn't need the money.

My co-worker and I attempted to arrive at a profound psychological reason as to why this person would continue to put up with such an unhappy situation. Finally, my friend sighed and said, "I guess we will have to write it off to the 'first law.'"

"What's that?" I asked curiously.

In a low voice, imitating a professor emeritus filled with wisdom, he said, "The law will never leave you."

Although I felt he was getting a little overdramatic, I have to admit he was *right*. The law has often explained to me why people form relationships with certain other people. It also has given me answers as to why people spend their time the way they do.

The first law, according to my psychiatrist friend, is that *the flow of money governs all behavior*. That is all there is to it. Although it is not long or complicated, I find it is disgustingly true. In essence, what this law says is that people's behavior is based largely upon whether they will get paid for it or whether it will cost them something. Money is at the basis of their behavior.

Of course, Scripture points out the futility of basing your happiness on money.

> He who loves silver will not be satisfied with silver;
> Nor he who loves abundance, with increase.
> This also is vanity.
> When goods increase,
> They increase who eat them;
> So what profit have the owners
> Except to see them with their eyes?
> The sleep of a laboring man is sweet,
> Whether he eats little or much;
> But the abundance of the rich will not permit him
> to sleep.[1]

The contemporary evangelical often experiences guilt related to having money and a feeling of virtue connected to living in poverty. Actually, this virtue may be a rationalization by the poor to help them accept their poverty more easily. The problem, however, is not in having money, but the stress involved in obtaining it.

The first step toward sin is to spend time obtaining money at the expense of time spent building relationships that are more important to us, starting with our walk with God. In the same way your marriage is affected by the love of money. Relationships suffer when they are neglected. Spending time earning money is one of the most common ways of neglecting your marriage.

On the other hand, if God has allowed you to be blessed with money and you have it in its proper place in your life, thank Him for it. Be good stewards, liberal givers, and enjoy it!

THE COST OF REORDERED PRIORITIES

There is a price attached to getting out of this double bind. Whether it is time, money, or some other force that is drawing you away from your marriage, to change it will cost you something. Are you willing to pay the price? One thing I should point out: If you choose to leave things as they are, there is also a price for that, and it will be far more costly.

For example, *Time* once reported:

> Pelé, Brazilian soccer hero, was separated from his wife Rose after twelve years of marriage and three children. His life has been filled with various commitments, including soccer camps and TV commercials that keep the retired soccer star on the road. Said Pelé, "I have been on the road for 22 years. Rose says it has to stop, *but I cannot*" [italics mine].[2]

After reading this, I am sure your mind runs to others closer to home in the same situation but with different demands.

A study on divorce reported by the *Minneapolis Star* stated that the parsonage is increasingly becoming "a place of marital conflict." The report attributed much of the marital breakdown to three essential parts of what the article called the clergy mystique: (1) high expectations of congregations, (2) fear of failure, and (3) the *time* they are expected to spend on church business.[3] Pastors, like everyone else, can get caught in this time trap.

As you can see, if you choose not to get out of this double bind, there is a high price to pay which can cost you your marriage.

Marriages often receive merely scraps of time left from schedules after everything else is done. One reason is that you live under the illusion that you are spending more time together than you really are, simply because you live under the same roof. Seeing each other only early in the morning and late in the evening is not enough to keep your marriage alive. In the morning we are preoccupied with the events that lie ahead for the day, and by evening we are tired and need to wind down. Whether we have been working outside or inside the home, our best time has been spent.

To begin giving time to your marriage you must take time from some other area of your life. The area you drop out of your schedule may be one you really enjoy, one that satisfies a great many of those needs that were previously unmet in your marriage.

Now the pressure is really on. What will you give up? Can you cut down on your overinvolvement in church without feeling guilty? Which Christian organization's board will you turn down to spend more time with your spouse? What about that hunting or fishing trip you planned? Will the women's club survive without your leadership? Are you willing to accept the cold rejection that may follow when you say no to that important position no one else can do as well?

How much money are you willing to give up earning in order to spend more time with your spouse? Will you decline that promotion because it requires more travel? Make the correct choice; only *you* can do it.

Let me tell you about one man who was faced with this problem and made his choice. Six months ago a veteran police officer and his wife came to me for counseling.

"I have had it!" she said angrily as she related the years she had felt like a widow. While her husband had been a "good" police officer, putting in long hours serving the community, she was on her way toward a divorce.

For six years her husband had been a police sergeant, which gave him status, signified by the stripes on his uniform, and an extra $300 a month in salary. The catch was that during the entire six-year period he was required to work the night shift while his wife worked a day job. They only saw each other on weekends, but by then the tension was already thick.

Before I could even suggest it, the husband told me he was giving up his sergeant's rank. This would shorten his hours and put him on a day shift.

"No amount of money is worth what that job is costing my marriage," he said. This man considered the price and chose to pay it. Today they are happy and $300 a month poorer—or are they really richer?

Everyone's price is different. Only you know what it will cost you to change. Just remember, the cost is greater if you choose not to change.

Here are some tested tools that will help you in your effort to get out of the double bind.

1. Determine before God that you are ready to make whatever changes are necessary, and trust Him to lead you in knowing what they are.
2. Establish your priority list. Let your spouse and children know what these priorities are. Live by them consistently.
3. In the area of relationship priorities I believe they should come in the following order:
   a. First and foremost, give top priority to your spiritual relationship with God. Be firmly in touch with His will for your life, and follow it.
   b. Your relationship with your marital partner comes next, and should receive the love, attention, care, and concern reserved for this most important human relationship.
   c. Next come your children. After your spouse, your children's needs must receive your attention as their parent and the one responsible for their care.
   d. Vocational and employment responsibilities are next. Although your career is often placed first in your life, it really belongs fourth.

(Following these four main priorities will come others unique to your lives. The list is arranged in this way because you must have a solid relationship with God before you can effectively relate to your spouse. In turn, you cannot adequately care for your children if your marriage is not in the right place. Likewise, your effectiveness on the job is directly related to the happiness and stability of your family life.)

4. Husbands and wives, discuss your finances and determine how important money is to you. Be honest. Often spouses never discuss money matters. Determine together the connection between the amount of money you need and the amount of time you are willing to give to earn it. Then make some decisions about time and money in your marriage.
5. In the same manner, discuss your time schedules. Rearrange them in such a way as to allow time to be alone individually with your children, and time to be alone as a couple. Then carefully protect this schedule so that outside influences do not erode it.
6. In the area of time management, here are some specific concrete suggestions that have proven successful for other couples. Perhaps they will also be helpful to you.
   a. Have at least one night a week as family night. Let absolutely nothing interfere with this time that has been set aside for your spouse and children. Some families vary the night from week to week. Be flexible.
   b. One night a week have dinner alone *as a couple*. Alternate between going out and staying home, depending upon your mood and the cash available. If you choose to eat at home, make it pleasant with china, candles, and music to set the atmosphere. No matter what you have on the menu, it doesn't cost any more to make it nice *just for the two of you*.
   c. Arrange to meet your spouse regularly for lunch or dinner. Spend some time together with good food and adult conversation.
   d. At least three or four times a year, leave your children and get away as a couple for a weekend. Place yourself in a setting away from your children, telephones, and all the other demands that come between you and the one you married. Devote this time to recharging your marriage.

I have given you four concrete suggestions that other couples have found extremely helpful in their marriages. Realizing that every marriage is unique, let me suggest you add a few more of your own.

Chapter Eleven

Every Married Person Needs an Affair

He traded in the station wagon for a sports car. The bald spot on his head was covered with a new hair piece, and he wore new tinted glasses. Some of his best friends did not recognize him. Fashionable, more expensive designer clothes replaced the usual drab suits he had worn for years. In addition to these not-so-subtle changes, he had become increasingly quiet and withdrawn around home. The changes had been happening for quite some time, but everyone was too busy to notice.

Then it finally hit. He told his wife he had been unhappy and needed to get away for a while to think, to spend some time alone. He rented a modest apartment on the other side of town. The address and telephone number remained secret because he needed to get away from everything, including her. But she could call him at the office.

Later she learned that the modest apartment was really a bachelor's pad, lavishly furnished in a style opposite from the conservative furnishings in their home.

Although no one had said anything yet, his friends and associates were noticing that he had lost interest in a business that had consumed his attention for years. Getting new clients was no longer important. He was coming to work later, leaving earlier, and his lunches were lasting up to two hours.

In the past he had often stayed at the office and eaten a bag lunch or had something sent in from the local sandwich shop.

Although all the evidences pointed toward it, no one really wanted to believe what was so contrary to the image he had portrayed all those years. But it was true; he was having an affair.

He stumbled over his words as he tried to explain to his wife how he and another woman had become such good friends. Even though she was young enough to be his daughter, he talked about her maturity and sensitivity to his needs.

"We enjoyed talking to each other and never expected it to be more than that," he continued.

He never did describe their arrangement as an affair. Usually no one involved does. Like the others, he said, "Ours is something different." He called it a special friendship and any other number of neutral labels, instead of facing up to what it really was: an affair, fornication, adultery.

Completely stunned by the revelation, his wife couldn't think at first. She was in shock. Every possible emotion rushed through her at lightning pace—confusion followed by anger, then sorrow. Thinking it over, she felt compassion for her husband and the confusion he must be experiencing. Then she was back to sheer anger again. Over and over her mind flip-flopped as she tried to grasp what was taking place.

WHO HAS AFFAIRS?

This story is not unique. It happens more often than most of us realize even though everyone who has an affair claims his or her story is different. It is happening all around you—yes, even to Christians.

Who has affairs? What are the people like? Contrary to what you may think, many are not basically immoral, irresponsible persons living a carefree lifestyle of satisfying their sensual desires. Actually, they are most often the opposite.

Solid and conservative people, they are leaders in the community, serving on committees and organizations that benefit all. They are the epitome of dependability—hard workers, sacrificing for the good of others. They are often active in church, holding at one time or another leadership positions. They are the last people in the world others would suspect. "Who would have believed it?" neighbors ask when the truth emerges.

People who fall into an affair of this type are often the ones who, in the past, were especially critical of others in similar situations. But now it has become a personal experience. "Why did you do it?" we ask. "What brought it about?"

Although there are almost as many answers to that question as persons who ask it, I believe there are some common reasons for most affairs.

Consider where these people are coming from. For years they have conscientiously denied their own needs and the needs of the marriage for other things. For years they have been busy doing for others, receiving the usual praise that reinforces their lifestyle and forces them even deeper into that behavior. Doing for others is good, but not if it gets out of balance.

If your marital needs are not being met, you are vulnerable and can fall into the clutches of an experience you will later pay for dearly. Most people who have an affair do not consciously go out looking for it. They just don't stop the affair when they see it coming. The longer they wait, the more difficult it is to stop.

One day it could happen to you. No one is immune. The setting and circumstances may vary, but the process is the same. Check out your feelings as you see how it happened to one person. His story is true.

"I was pleasantly surprised when she brought in that hot cup of coffee late in the afternoon, especially when I hadn't asked for it. She must have known it had been an extra long day for me, and it wasn't over yet. The report I was working on was full of corrections and it was too late to have it retyped that afternoon.

"It was already six and only a couple of office staff were still around. Somehow she knew I wanted to work further on the report; she offered to stay late and retype it if I could drop her off at her apartment. Her friend, who had driven that day, was ready to leave and couldn't wait. I was more than happy to return the favor to get the freshly typed report. Her apartment was only a mile or two out of my way, and I had nothing special planned that night at home.

"Finishing the report, I quickly packed my briefcase and together we closed up the office. The empty corridor echoed from our footsteps as we laughed and chatted on our way toward the parking ramp. Although I had been exhausted most of the day, I didn't feel tired now. I couldn't figure out when this surge of energy had come, but it really felt good.

"She seemed so vibrant and alive. I had forgotten how, when you're young and single, you can turn off the cares of the job when you walk out the door at night. It was apparent that she could do it, and it had a contagious effect on me. For a moment I forgot I was a vice president facing a tough board meeting the next day. I also forgot I had a wife and three children at home, one with a fever when I had left that morning. I forgot it all for the moment.

"Following her instructions, I turned right as we pulled out of the ramp and headed down the boulevard. Even that was a change. For years the car had automatically turned left, taking the usual route home. She snapped on the radio, turning it to her favorite station, and started to sing along with the music. Although I didn't know the words, I found myself humming and tapping the steering wheel right along with the rhythm.

"Turning left off the boulevard, we went around a little park, past a shopping center, and into a modest complex of apartment buildings. She pointed to her building, and I pulled up in front. We sat for a moment looking into each other's eyes. It was one of those uncomfortable times when it seemed that each of us was waiting for the other to speak. I broke the silence by thanking her for what she had done for me that night. She thought I meant the report, and so did I. But in reality I knew later it was for what I had felt that evening with her.

"Driving away, I continued to leave the radio tuned to the same station, filling the car with her music. I now realize I was trying to make the feelings last as long as possible. Why, I hadn't felt that way in years. I was excited, happy, alive, and young again. These feelings really felt good, but they were frightening because they were so strong. The thought that this was wrong entered my head for only a moment. Then it left as I rationalized: How could feeling so good be wrong?

"As I drove into our neighborhood, reality started to settle in. The rows of large, expensive houses with their carefully manicured lawns stood as monuments of judgment to our great professional success. They were too perfect to be homes. There was also a competitive conformity that no one ever admitted mattered to them. Waving to a couple of neighbors from my open car window, I quickly changed the radio station. I was now embarrassed at the music still playing and didn't want them to hear it.

"I met my wife pulling out of the driveway as I drove in. She smiled and I waved. She was late for her women's auxiliary, and this year she was president.

"The last of my good feelings left me as I entered my monument and sat down alone at the table for dinner. Everyone else had gone to one thing or another, except my oldest son who was still in bed with a slight fever. In her usual thoughtful way, my wife had kept dinner warm in the oven for me.

"Next to my plate was the customary note from my wife with a list of things that needed my attention while she was gone. She is a strong, well-organized woman whom I respect very much. Yes, I do respect and admire her, but any other feelings are pretty much dead.

"After dinner, I checked on my son who was sleeping and did the tasks on my list. Then I settled into my chair to study the report for tomorrow's meeting. I knew I was in trouble as

I tried to concentrate on the contents but found myself thinking instead of the woman who had typed it. The feelings were back, and I wanted to see her."

This gentleman told me that this is how the whole thing started. He never had any intention of having an affair, but he did. The seed of desire was planted and one thing led to another. There were more late afternoon cups of coffee and reports to be typed at the last minute. This meant more trips by her apartment and eventually invitations to come in. Then there were picnics and secret lunches. Notes and glances were discreetly exchanged in the office. Then the bubble broke. She wanted to know when he intended to tell his wife and get a divorce. She wanted to tell her friends about her plans for marriage.

He didn't have to tell his wife. She already suspected something. Finally, she confronted him. He admitted the whole thing, almost relieved to do so. His wife was hurt, but what really shook her up was the fact that he wasn't sure he wanted to give up the affair.

THAT "IN-LOVE" FEELING

That "in-love" feeling is what confuses everyone, especially those involved in the affair. The feelings are so strong that even after the infidelity is discovered they may still want to continue the extramarital relationship in spite of the cost to themselves and others.

How often the innocent party will ask me, "How can my spouse possibly feel he is in love when he barely knows the person?" Usually affairs happen quickly. My answer to them is that they are not "in love" with a *person,* but with a *feeling* they haven't experienced for years.

This is borne out as I listen to them tell me about the new relationship. They do not talk much about the person, but go on and on about how they feel when they are with the other person. Any reference to the person is usually connected to that wonderful feeling they get when they are together.

People having affairs are not reluctant to give up the person. They are reluctant to give up those feelings—that experience of being alive and finding the excitement of love again.

Sitting in my office, one man told me he had never been so confused in all his life. Being an executive, he had always been good at making decisions; this time he could not seem to do it. He looked at me and said, "I hadn't felt so good in years, yet now I feel good and bad. I'm confused! Why does an affair have to be so bad when it makes you feel so good?"

He almost fell off his chair when I told him I thought every married person ought to have an affair. From the shocked look on his face I was sure he was preparing himself to hear some type of open-marriage solution to their problem. What I told him was very different, but it was the solution to an extramarital affair with its powerful, potentially destructive force. Affairs are deceptive. They destroy individuals, careers, certainly marriages, and families. Anyone close to the person involved in an affair is affected.

Problems arise when someone has an affair with the wrong person. Have an affair, but have it with your spouse. Create situations to give you good feelings, but let your husband or wife be your partner. This removes the conflict that leads to destruction and allows the good feelings to remain. An extramarital affair is wrong because it is sin. It produces infidelity, adultery, and lies. No amount of rationalization can change what God says: "Marriage is honorable among all, and the bed undefiled; but fornicators and adulterers God will judge."[1]

The benefit of an affair is the change in lifestyle from overemphasis on the rigid controls and expectations of others to becoming more sensitive to your own emotional needs. You have every right to feel young and alive again. Just find those feelings with your spouse, not with someone else. Then you will be guilt-free and have God's blessings. Also, some interesting changes often happen to your spouse, as with the man having an affair, whose story appeared earlier in the chapter.

His wife made a decision to love him back into the marriage, and it worked. The Bible has told us that love is even greater than faith and hope. "And now abide faith, hope, love, these three; but the greatest of these is love."[2] When you are confused and don't know what to do, try loving. You can't go wrong. But you must stick with it.

In loving her husband back into the marriage, the wife realized that some changes needed to be made on her part. She abandoned the usual list that accompanied his evening meal. She turned some of the women's auxiliary duties over to her assistant chairman and began to meet her husband downtown frequently after work for dinner. Sometimes they never made it home but ended their evening by staying overnight at a hotel. To his amazement, he began feeling alive, but this time with his wife. Best of all there was no sin, no lies, no infidelity, and no guilt.

Later his wife confessed that in all honesty his affair with the secretary had in some ways helped their marriage and had helped her as an individual. She made it clear that it was still wrong and she would not wish it on anyone, not even her worst enemy. But it did force them to look at their life together and get straight what is really important. Spending a night at a hotel is far more fun than attending every auxiliary meeting. Her parting comment to me was, "I just wish all married couples could learn what we did, *without* the affair and the pain that accompanied it."

Chapter Twelve

Confession/Forgiveness: The Only Road to Restoration

Summer has truly arrived in Minnesota when the warm July breezes fill the air. Sick of winter, everyone tries to cut back their workload and get to one of our ten thousand lakes for sun and recreation. I was no different. After a full week of appointments I was counting the hours until my family and I could head for the water. We had been invited by friends to spend the weekend at their cottage.

I had gained professional success and was sensing the security and pride of being in demand by numerous referral sources for my skill and service in counseling. My professional network included two medical clinics, a full-time affiliation with the largest psychiatric clinic in Minneapolis, faculty positions with two colleges, and a full speaking schedule for churches, retreats, and seminars. Furthermore, the manuscript for my third book was nearing completion.

Our family also seemed especially close after returning from a wonderful three-week tour through the West. It had been one of those trips every family should take before their children are grown and move away. Our creativity had really exploded as we produced a family movie of the trip entitled "How the West Was Won, Part II, by the Dahl Family." However, we discovered the five of us were the only ones who could endure watching the entire, full-length feature, which exceeded three hours.

Every family member was anticipating the coming school year. Peter would be entering his last year of high school with all of the honors and recognitions that make it such a special year in the life of a senior. Within a year our family would experience the normal disruptions of a first-born leaving the nest for college. But this was to be the summer when everything was still in place, predictable and secure.

That Friday in July 1982, I was seeing clients at the satellite office of our clinic. An extra appointment had been squeezed in, so I still had one more session before our family could leave for our weekend vacation. In the middle of this next-to-last session my telephone buzzed, an unusual interruption since the receptionist allowed only urgent calls to interfere with a counseling situation. The call was from one of my closest colleagues at the clinic.

"Jerry, sorry to interrupt your session, but I'm just leaving the clinic for the lake and will be gone all next week. I felt it was necessary to reach you before I left."

"What's up?" I inquired.

"The clinic administrator and I met today with a lawyer from St. Paul. He informed us that a client you saw in therapy a couple years ago . . ."

My heart started to pound and a knot formed in my stomach as he said the client's name. I knew what was coming. In silence, I continued to listen to the painful message.

"The lawyer told us this client alleges that unethical behavior occurred during your therapy relationship. A legal action is being considered. Isn't this the craziest thing you've ever heard?"

I muttered some kind of affirmative response. Yet I knew differently. I remembered that time in my life two years earlier, and now the pain resurfaced. I realized I would have to face openly and publicly something I had tried to keep to myself. At the time, I privately confessed my wrongdoing to the Lord and transferred the client to another therapist. I had hoped this matter would be buried in my past.

"I'll talk to you after I get back from vacation," he continued. "We'll plan our strategy then."

"Thanks for calling so promptly," I said quietly.

Hanging up the telephone, I walked across the room to resume therapy. Fortunately, my client carried the rest of the session as my mind became numb with the preoccupation of the message I had just received. As the session closed, I escorted my client to the waiting room to schedule the next appointment. Silently, I wondered, how many future appointments would there be for me to offer in this setting or anywhere.

The receptionist apologetically said, "Jerry, I'm sorry for interrupting your session, but the doctor said the matter was urgent."

"That's okay, I needed to talk to him," I replied.

Somehow I muddled through my last session. Although everything was still in place, life for me had suddenly become tentative and uncertain.

Peter stopped by to switch cars. He had a date and looked terrific. Happy and on top of the world as any seventeen-year-old senior on summer break should be, I wondered what would happen when he learned the truth. He took the new car and went on his way.

I took my time driving home that night, trying to sort out the meaning of what I had learned in the past two hours. I recalled my relationship with that client and what had happened to bring about those allegations. She and her husband had chosen me to counsel them because they said I was warm and caring. Along with the caring were the hugs we all had given each other. This is an expression of care that no longer has a place in the professional counseling relationship, especially behind the closed doors of the counselor's office. There are many professional ways of expressing care without physically touching, which can lead to serious consequences.

But somewhere in the course of this particular therapy relationship, I had not heeded that advice. My physical expression of care crossed over those appropriate limits, and I knew I had violated the ethical standards. Fear and guilt immediately entered my life and caused me not to talk to anyone about what had happened. I had sensed some resolution to what had occurred with the client as we terminated therapy. With the situation almost two years behind me I had begun to sense some relief—until today.

Pulling into the driveway, I waved to Judy, who was painting the trim around the kitchen window. This had become her project since returning from our California vacation. She was excited to show me what she had accomplished.

I tried to soak up some of her happiness, but my deep inner sadness shut it out. A private wall of emotional distance was forming, and I knew all joy was soon to disappear when the crisis became known.

For over two weeks I said nothing about what I was facing. After the first meeting at the clinic about the incident, I told Judy about the allegations. Her response was the same as that of the others—she assumed my innocence. Not being pressed for a direct answer, I continued to let my silence imply that I was blameless.

However, as time passed, a new guilt was growing. I knew my silence was communicating a lie of innocence. Confession must come, but when and how? Several months passed and meetings continued with various officials regarding legal strategies. Then, one cold winter weekend early in January 1983, I came to the end of myself.

In one of my darkest hours, alone with the Lord, I said to Him, "Why live?" I was not suicidal, but I could no longer see a purpose for my life, believing that my career could be over with my confession. The Lord's response to me, as clearly as if He had said it audibly, was, "Jerry, it is time that you do die." Seeking some meaning to what I was sensing, I read Matthew 16:25: "For whoever desires to save his life will lose it, and whoever loses his life for My sake will find it."

All of my efforts to build a career and save it now seemed futile. According to that verse, the key to truly saving one's life was to lose it. I had searched for alternatives in a futile effort to preserve some dignity. Now I saw that the roots of my effort were in pride and concern for hurting the ones I loved. Now it was time to abandon it all to Christ and let Him do through me what I had failed to accomplish through my own efforts for Him.

Confession is painful. What I was about to do would be the most difficult step in my entire life. After a sleepless night with the last remnants of self struggling to avoid this painful step, I watched the bedroom fill with the rising sun. Judy opened her eyes as she sensed me staring at her.

"Have you been awake long?" she asked.

"Most of the night," I replied. "Honey, there is some truth in the allegations." My heart was pounding, not knowing what would happen next.

After talking further, Judy replied, "Jerry, now *we* have a problem." My greatest fear seemed to have become a reality as this crisis attacked our marriage. Yet within moments I quickly learned that the opposite was true. Judy, through tears, assured me of her continued love. What had been my problem to carry alone was now ours to share. From that moment I was no longer alone. Judy was by my side, and together, we faced the crisis.

Individually and privately, I discussed the problem with each of the children and in turn, received their love and support. Then, together, we talked as a family. Peter the oldest, accompanied me on occasion to the numerous meetings where I had to explain the matter. Family became my greatest base of human support. By losing my life, I was now finding it. Matthew 16:25 really worked!

During the months that followed major changes occurred in every aspect of my life. Every anchor of professional security that I had nurtured over the years vanished. My positions with the clinics and colleges were terminated. A book manuscript was shelved. Many long-standing relationships with colleagues and friends disappeared in the turmoil of my crisis. I was unemployed and without human direction.

Now I understand why the Lord needed to take me

through these darkest hours. Only after everything of human value was gone, could I truly discover the full presence and power of Christ in my life. The Scriptures spoke with new enlightenment: "In Him was life, and the life was the light of men. And the light shines in the darkness, and the darkness did not comprehend it."[1]

Light came from Christ through His Word. Along with the spiritual presence of the Lord, Judy and our three children were there. The commitment of unconditional love was working. For the next six weeks Judy and I remained at home and daily spent hours with the Lord, praying and reading the Scriptures. Confession is a beginning, but restoration is a process. Not knowing the future, we had embarked on a life of faith.

The events which followed could fill a book. But the details of the crises in my life are not what matter here. Instead, I desire to clearly show you the steps you can take when you face a crisis and desire restoration.

As you read the account of my crisis, you may be recalling your own. You need to know that the road of confession and forgiveness is one I have personally walked. It is the only road to recovery when relationships are marred and broken by sin.

Initially, we desperately search for alternatives that can somehow help us save face and preserve our old dignity. This is the first course I chose when I tried to bury my sin after it had been confessed only to God. But that was not enough. Confession must also be made to one another. And that is part of the process of dying to self.

Pride and self-devised solutions cause us to seek less painful alternatives. Searching for self-understanding apart from God leads us away from true restoration. As Oswald Chambers wrote:

> The only One who understands us is God. The greatest curse in spiritual life is conceit. If we have ever had a glimpse of what we are like in the sight of God, we shall never say, "Oh, I am

> so unworthy," because we shall know we are, beyond the possibility of stating it. As long as we are not quite sure that we are unworthy, God will keep narrowing us in until He gets us alone.[2]

The presence of pride or conceit in our lives blocks the Lord from doing His work of restoration. True confession removes that pride. Look into the spiritual mirror of the Word of God and discover the required walk of restoration when sin enters our lives.

THE PROMISE

The Word of God promises hope in what appears to be a hopeless situation. Walk through the Scriptures with me as we travel the road of confession and forgiveness leading to restoration. But a new road requires a map to follow. The following is the road map to recovery taken directly from the Scriptures.

> The steps of a *good* man are ordered by the LORD,
> And He delights in his way.
> Though he fall, he shall not be utterly cast down;
> For the LORD upholds *him with* His hand.
> I have been young, and *now* am old;
> Yet I have not seen the righteous forsaken,
> Nor his descendants begging bread.[3]

There is something comforting about King David's witness as he reflects on his lifelong walk with the Lord during his latter years. David had experienced the mountaintops of success, having been used of the Lord from his early youth when he slayed the giant, Goliath, with a sling. David had also faced the darkest despair when he was confronted by Nathan with the sin of his adultery with Bathsheba.[4]

All people, including King David, are capable of falling into sin. Our success in earthly terms does not protect us. I recall one particularly helpful session I had while seeking spiritual counsel during my restoration. A wise counselor pointed out that we are often safely on guard in the areas of predictable vulnerability. Falling usually does not take place there but, instead, where we think we are the strongest. I fell in the counseling office, the absolute last place I would have expected to slip.

If this has also happened to you, there is hope. You will not be cast down, even though every human support seems to be removed. The Lord will uphold you with His hand. He will also send others to support you.

Galatians 6:1, 2 states, "Brethren, if a man is overtaken in any trespass, you who *are* spiritual restore such a one in a spirit of gentleness, considering yourself lest you also be tempted. Bear one another's burdens, and so fulfill the law of Christ." The word *overtaken* implies a fall similar to that of a runner in a race who falls in an unforeseen hole in the road. The fall is unexpected, awkward, and often the runner is cut and bruised. The key is that the fall occurs when his eyes are taken off the road.

The lesson is clear that a disciplined walk of obedience is essential to keep from falling. The other message in this important passage is that restoration is provided through godly people's supporting and being a part of the process.

CONFESSION TO GOD—THE KEY TO FORGIVENESS

"If we confess our sins, He is faithful and just to forgive us our sins and to cleanse us from all unrighteousness."[5]

Confession begins with the Lord. The word *confess* means "to be in agreement with God."[6] At first that agreement may be difficult to admit. Our rationalization and system of denial keeps deceiving us into believing that our situation is different. As long as the consequences are not fully realized, we tend to call the matter that needs confession anything but what it really is—sin. This stance creates distance and strain in all our relationships.

Look into the spiritual mirror of 1 John 1:10, "If we say that we have not sinned, we make Him a liar, and His word is not in us." Confession is the beginning of true honesty.

Satan's hold on us is trampled as the shackles of self-effort are loosed and we experience the beginning strength of the Lord in our lives.

Many people with whom I have counseled tell me they have made this confession, but still feel bound inside. Although confession is never an easy task, the confession to God in the privacy of our prayer life is often viewed as the safest. We are tempted to stop at that point, secretly hoping we will not have to go any further. This is what I experienced for more than a year before my sin became known to others. However, we confess to God for the *forgiveness of sin,* but that is only the first step on the road to recovery.

CONFESSION TO ONE ANOTHER—THE KEY TO HEALING

"Confess your trespasses to one another, and pray for one another, that you may be healed."[7] Confession to God provides forgiveness but healing requires confession to one another. Now the road gets tougher. Honestly facing our sin before God is difficult. But to look directly into the eyes of those closest to us and to confess our wrongdoing is a supreme hurdle.

In this confession process we get a clear impact of the hurt and pain our fall has had on others. One of the most painful parts of this process is to observe the sadness in the eyes of those whom we care about as we tell them what we've done. When your life is devoted to the removing of emotional pain from others' lives, as mine is by profession, you can begin to imagine how hard it was to have done something that gave so much pain to others.

However, to realize that the pain was caused by the sin, not by the confession, allows us to be frank and honest. And the hurt felt in confession will diminish as the relationship heals and truth becomes the new basis for the relationship.

The fifth step in the Alcoholics Anonymous program recognizes the power of confession in the healing process. Those in treatment recall the hurts they have caused others by their chemical abuse. Then they make a confession to a selected person. I have been that selected person for several who have taken the fifth step in the program. Let me assure you, confession is never an easy process.

The difficulty of confession is partially tied to the possibility of rejection. Ideally, this should not happen, but sometimes it does. Although the risk of rejection must be realized, it must not keep you from confession.

We do not know for certain what will happen to our relationships when we confess a sin. Although the Lord's presence and faithfulness are always sure and true, people are frail and unpredictable. We never know what their response will be.

Contrary to my original belief, I have learned that confession does not usually create problems in relationships. Instead, it exposes problems that already existed. True commitment is put to the supreme test. Confession will either cause the relationship to dissolve or cause the commitment to emerge on a solid foundation. Are you ready to take the risk?

CONFESSION—TRUE OR FALSE?

You may say that you have confessed to God. You have also told your spouse and selected others that you are sorry. However, nothing really seems to have changed. You have not found joy. Your spouse still has reservations about forgiving you. Something is missing, but there doesn't seem to be anything left for you to do. How do you pass this roadblock?

First, we should recognize that not all confessions are sincere. Confession requires more than words; it involves the condition of the heart. Let's look closely at three confessions. Two did not receive forgiveness, but the third did.

FALSE CONFESSION #1

In Exodus 9:27 Pharaoh called for Moses and Aaron saying, "I have sinned this time." Here we have a confession. Pharaoh told Moses that he had sinned before God. The confession was made, but God did not forgive Pharaoh. Why?

FALSE CONFESSION #2

As we look at the life of King Saul in 1 Samuel 13, we read about his unlawful sacrifice of the burnt offering. Saul later said to Samuel:

> "I have sinned, for I have transgressed the commandment of the LORD and your words, because I feared the people and obeyed their voice. Now therefore, please pardon my sin, and return with me, that I may worship the LORD."
>
> But Samuel said to Saul, "I will not return with you, for you have rejected the word of the LORD, and the LORD has rejected you from being king over Israel"[8]

There was no forgiveness for Saul's confession. Why?

TRUE CONFESSION #3

Most of us are familiar with the Old Testament story of David and Bathsheba. While walking one night on his roof, David observed a woman bathing and saw that she was very beautiful. Here was the temptation. He asked about the woman, and after learning she was the wife of one of his generals, Uriah, who was away at war, he proceeded to act on the temptation and invited her to dinner. They had sexual intercourse, and she conceived a child.

Caught in the trap of an extramarital affair, David tried to cover his sin. He called Bathsheba's husband home, believing Uriah would sleep with Bathsheba and later believe he was responsible for her pregnancy. The plan was foiled by the loyalty of Uriah to his army. He refused to sleep with his wife, but, instead, slept with the servants at the door of the king's house.

David then arranged for Uriah to go to the front of the hottest battle, knowing he would be killed. After Uriah's death, David took Bathsheba into his house, and she became his wife. What had happened displeased the Lord. So He sent Nathan, who confronted David through a parable.

"You are the man!" Nathan exclaimed in 2 Samuel 12:7. Then, David confessed, " 'I have sinned against the LORD.' And Nathan said to David, 'The LORD also has put away your sin; you shall not die' "[9]

David was forgiven! Why? We find the answer in Psalm 51, David's prayer of repentance.

First, he acknowledged that his sin was against the Lord. "Against You, You only, have I sinned."[10] So often we forget that we break God's laws when we sin. We must first be reconciled with our Lord, without regard to how we stand with other people. Losing our close, conscious walk with the Lord is a key element whenever we fall, and it must be re-established before we can go on.

Second, David revealed to us the elements of a confession acceptable to God. Let's read it together in Psalm 51:

> For You do not desire sacrifice, or else I would give it;
> You do not delight in burnt offering.
> The sacrifices of God are a broken spirit,
> A broken and a contrite heart—
> These, O God, You will not despise.[11]

A confession acceptable to God and to another must be more than words. It must come from a heart that is sorrowful and grieving over the sin that has saddened the heart of the Lord and others. This is the confession that God hears and forgives. Anything less is insufficient for it minimizes the reality of sin, and our sincere desire to be one with the Lord.

Waves of sadness continued during the weeks following my confession to Judy, as the Scriptures clearly revealed my life through spiritual eyes. Oswald Chambers said:

> Unless we get hurt right out of every deception about ourselves, the work of God is not having its way with us. The Word of God hurts as no sin can ever hurt because sin blunts feeling. It hurts not only in the natural way but in the profound personal way until there is no deception left.[12]

Looking back at Pharaoh's confession, we read, "And when Pharaoh saw that the rain, the hail, and the thunder had ceased, he sinned yet more."[13] And in King Saul's situation we read, "I have sinned, . . . Now, therefore, please pardon my sin, and return with me."[14] Both Pharaoh and Saul said the words, but their hearts were insincere. They confessed primarily to put themselves back in an acceptable place with those around them. A sincere confession from a broken heart puts self to death. Then reconciliation takes place and relationships are restored.

ONE FINAL STEP TO CONFESSION

The word *penance* often appears in the confession process. This means to agree with God and under the authority of the church that you have sinned. A second word *penitence* implies one's sorrow over the sin. One can acknowledge penance without being penitent, as reflected by Pharaoh and Saul when they cried, "I have sinned."

In penitence, with a broken and contrite heart, David expressed a deep, sincere sorrow for his sin. This ingredient was unique to David's confession and made him worthy of forgiveness.

The completion of confession involves one final step—repentance. This is the sincere and earnest desire not to sin again. In 2 Chronicles 7:14 we read: "If My people who are called by My name will humble themselves, and pray and seek My face, and turn from their wicked ways, then I will hear from heaven, and will forgive their sin and heal their land."

Restoration requires that you humble yourself, pray, seek God's face, and *turn from you wicked ways*. Repentance means that you exercise your will to turn from sin. Time after time in the counseling session, couples talk about asking God to take a certain sin out of their life. They are disillusioned when their prayer does not seem to be answered and they continue in that sin.

As weak and feeble as our efforts may be, we must first exercise our desire not to sin. Consider the first impulse in attitude or behavior that leads you into sin, and resist at that point. Often people play with temptation in its initial stages, and by the time they attempt to resist, they are too far into the sin.

A person who has been tempted to frequent pornographic bookstores needs, with his prayer of deliverance, to choose not to drive near that neighborhood. The alcoholic similarly must avoid situations where he or she may strongly desire to take that first drink.

When we resist, the Lord will hear our prayers and respond. It is an act of faith. Faith means action without evidence. We take the first step, believing. Then the Lord heals. This is repentance, the final act of confession.

FORGIVENESS—THE REQUIRED RESPONSE FROM THE OTHER SIDE

What is the response of those who receive the confession? Healing is always a two-way process involving both spouses. Once confession is offered, forgiveness must follow. Some spouses have told me they cannot seem to forgive. When this block occurs, the confession must be further examined. The problem is often not an unforgiving heart but rather an insincere confession.

All too often words may be loosely said in an effort to get the accuser off your back. "I'm sorry, now leave me alone!" is the type of insincere confession that cannot draw forgiveness. You must feel the pain you have caused the person to whom you are confessing. This is never easily done.

When confession is not offered from a broken heart, forgiveness is impossible. Confession must come first as we read in 1 John 1:9, "*If* we confess." Forgiveness from God is appropriated to us only if we are open to receiving it. Confession creates this openness.

Once a sincere confession is offered, a response of forgiveness is required. *For the believer who lives by the authority of the Scriptures, forgiveness is not an option*. It completes the healing process. Let's look at the words of our Lord: "For *if* you forgive men their trespasses, your heavenly Father will also forgive you. But *if* you do not forgive men their trespasses, neither will your Father forgive your trespasses" (italics mine).[15]

Again we see that little word *if* defining the condition for forgiveness. To receive forgiveness from the Father you must have a forgiving heart toward others. Paul, in his letter to the Colossians, wrote, "Bearing with one another, and forgiving one another, if anyone has a complaint against another; even as Christ forgave you, so you also must do."[16]

Many have asked Judy how she could forgive so quickly and completely in our situation? And I have often heard her answer that to look at the person or the confession alone is not enough. But when you view yourself at the foot of the cross as a forgiven person, your forgiveness flows as a natural response.

If forgiveness were based upon the eloquence of the spouse's confession, the door to conceit and self-centeredness would again be wide open because of one's fine confession. As Judy has stated, *"The only basis for us to offer forgiveness is because we too have been forgiven by God through Christ's work on the cross."* What you have received in forgiveness, freely give to the one who confesses to you. This is love expressed in the fullest sense.

My life will never be the same again. I view sin with a new seriousness. Service to the Lord is a cherished privilege. One person expressed how marvelous it was to see how I am continuing to trust the Lord. Although that is true, the marvelous fact is that He still trusts me to serve Him as a counselor and teacher. I believe that I will never fail again in this way, but I live my life as if it could happen every day.

Recalling the advice of one of my mentors, I am most cautious where I believe I am the strongest. There is now a window in the door of my counseling office, as well as the four offices of the associates who are part of our active facility. Although I cannot recall anyone looking through that window, it serves as a statement that nothing occurs in our offices that needs to be concealed from the eyes of another.

Each day this new walk is filled with evidence that the Lord is my Shepherd.

There is, however, a conclusion to the opening of this chapter. Following my confession, events reflecting the leading of the Lord took place. Restoration transpired through meetings of confession with others and a walk of obedience. Time with the Lord in reading and prayer has become a daily necessity as much as breathing. The legal matter was settled without litigation, a counseling office was reestablished, and wonderful new relationships developed with both old and new friends.

The healing power of Christ has been brought into the counseling process with a fresh boldness. Lives are being changed. What I once had attempted and failed to do for the Lord, He is doing now through Judy and me as a team. We have discovered what Hudson Taylor termed "the exchanged life in Christ."[17] We no longer live for self, for we have died to self that He may live in us and do His will through us.

This is the message we shared in churches as we presented the "exchanged life" in a seminar series. During the summer of 1984—two years after the telephone call that ignited the crisis, bringing to an end my old life—I was in the midst of a seminar where, unknowingly to me, the stage was being set for a public confession.

Two segments of a four-part series had been presented to a local church. Although the pastor of this church was aware of the crisis that had brought about my exchanged life, I had not announced or confessed it openly to the public.

I had previously wondered if the Lord would require a form of public confession in my restoration. Spiritual counsel had advised me to wait and let events dictate. Such was the case as I lectured on abandonment in the process of discovering the exchanged life. "You must die to yourself and whatever anyone may think of you so that Christ may be seen clearly in your new life," I said to the group in attendance at the Sunday meeting.

Little did I know, that very week I would personally be required to take another step in the abandonment process. July 1984, one year after a final committee meeting to handle the professional process of dealing with the crisis, an article appeared in the local newspaper reporting the allegations and the action of the committee. Again, the crisis was rekindled and the pain was fresh as a new group of individuals experienced the knowledge of my past.

Although love and support flowed from the leadership, the church where I was speaking felt it necessary to call a special board meeting to determine what course of action should be taken with regard to the continuation of the series. Even though we were not members of this church, the body of believers consisted of people we knew and loved in the Lord. The evening the article appeared, Judy and I met with the board. After a time of questioning, sharing, and praying, we were excused while the board determined if the series should continue.

In a bold act of faith and obedience, the church made its decision. Later that evening the telephone rang, and the pastor relayed the message: "Jerry, we unanimously voted for you to continue the series. We believe nothing has changed in the eyes of the Lord. Now more people know details of your crisis and what the Lord is doing in your life. Say whatever the Lord lays on your heart. We will be praying."

I thanked him and hung up the phone. By the courage of this church in their obedience to the Lord, a public forum had been created for my confession. Although they expected some of the time to be devoted to the continuation of the series, I knew that this entire session would be on a different subject. The will of God had been made known.

I arose early on that Sunday morning to spend time in prayer before the session. The presence of the Lord was giving me peace. I sensed anticipation, realizing this would bring closure to a period in my life and a confession-forgiveness process I had undergone daily for more than two years.

The parking lot seemed unusually full as we arrived for the

adult seminar that was offered during the Sunday school hour. Walking into the church, I found the attendance had increased significantly because of the newspaper article. After a time of prayer with the pastor in his study, we made our way to the front of the sanctuary. The pastor gave a brief introduction, and I walked to the podium.

A hush fell over the congregation. People were unusually attentive to what was about to be said. For a moment I paused to look at all the familiar faces. I seemed to recognize almost everyone. Most of them I had counseled with or taught at one time or another. These people deserved a confession, and now the opportunity to make my confession public had come in this church.

Scanning the audience one more time, I saw Tom, my good friend and brother in Christ. The presence of Christ had been made real to me through Tom's loving and ongoing support during the past two years. I asked him to pray that what was about to be said would reflect transparency and openness before the Lord. Then I spoke:

"Many of you I recognize from sessions we have had in my counseling office. Others are familiar with me from the classroom or the seminar lecture hall. And then there are those of you whom I have never met. Each of you has personal reasons for being here today.

"Counselors can give, with relative ease, advice to clients as we sit behind the security of our desks with our professional armour. The professor can teach the student with the same protection of his lectern. In most learning experiences you are told the principles and encouraged to follow them. This learning experience will be different. Today, I cannot tell you what to do. Instead, I must show you by stepping out from behind this podium and living the lesson that needs to be taught.

"This week many of you read an article in the newspaper about unethical behavior in my past professional life. There is truth in that report, which I deeply regret. Now I ask for your forgiveness."

I talked about the deceptiveness of sin and how no one is

above falling. Likewise, there is no exception on the road to restoration that one can take whether teacher or student, counselor or client, pastor or parishioner. Emotions were strong as many in the audience saw in me what I had seen in so many of them during our counseling sessions together.

Sin always brings pain. Hope and joy, however, return as the witness of the healing work of Christ is made clear. My entire family, several staff members from our counseling office, and other close associates and friends confirmed my witness that day.

The hour passed, and I offered a closing benediction. A fear came over me briefly as people stood to leave. I didn't know what they would do. For a moment I stood alone at the front, waiting. Then I became aware that few persons were leaving. Instead, they were moving toward me, forming lines in the three aisles. One by one, they embraced me, and we shared the love of Christ. Speaking with several, I discovered that the emotion they were feeling was not primarily for my confessed sin, but instead for theirs that needed confession.

That day many discovered that the church can be a safe place to make confession and receive forgiveness. Praise God!

Chapter Thirteen

The Power of Submission

The neighbors frequently heard shouting and quarreling from George and Claire's house, especially on warm summer days when the windows were open. Today was one of those times, and they were at it again.

"Don't tell me what to do!" Claire shouted defiantly.

"Someone competent around here, like me, has to take charge!" George shouted back.

"Get out of the Dark Ages, George," Claire yelled. "This is a different age from the days of your parents!"

"That's a matter of opinion, Claire! I can show you chapter and verse right out of the Bible where I can put you in the place you belong as a woman!"

The circumstances varied, but the pattern was always the same—a fight for control in the relationship. George was a "man's man." He owned a construction business and ran several crews as an army sergeant would. He drove a heavy duty, four-wheel-drive pickup truck, had the biggest power boat on the lake, and rode a 1000 cc motorcycle just for kicks. He took charge and controlled everything except Claire, his wife.

Claire was unique, with her own strand of stubborn independence. That was one of the main reasons George loved her as deeply as he did. In spite of her petite frame, she could turn up the volume and hold her own during the couple's frequent arguments. This time, however, they seemed to have passed the point of no return. Divorce threats had been introduced into the arsenal of weapons. At the peak of their fighting, Claire grabbed a small bag of clothes, her household checkbook, and announced she was leaving.

"Great! Good riddance!" replied George. "Don't let the door hit you from behind."

"Goodbye, George," Claire said with finality as she made her exit.

The door slammed. The roar of the engine and the squeal of the tires made a clear statement of Claire's feelings as she disappeared down the road. Suddenly, all was silent.

George stood in the kitchen for a long time. Bewildered and exhausted, he asked himself, *What happened?* He realized how difficult it was to think and shout at the same time. Now that Claire was gone and the shouting had stopped, George started to think.

What if she really doesn't return? he thought. The important part Claire played in his life came back into focus. *If she doesn't return, what will I do? Why do we fight all the time?* George's head was spinning with confused thoughts and feelings. Tears flowed down his cheeks. He didn't know what to do next.

Then his eyes caught the dirty marks on the kitchen floor. It seemed the floor was always a mess but he believed that scrubbing the kitchen floor was "wife's work." He wouldn't think of lowering himself to touch a scrub brush. But Claire also hated that dirty, thankless job, so it seldom was done.

Through tear-filled eyes, he continued to stare at the floor as he prayed, *Lord, what should I do?* Then came the message loud and clear: *Scrub the floor*. Grabbing a scrub brush, he began to funnel his emotional energy into vigorous scrubbing. The dirty marks on the kitchen tile disappeared.

In the meantime, Claire was also beginning to think clearly. Alone in the car, she asked herself, *What am I really trying to do?* Lost in her thoughts, she paused longer than usual after the light turned green. The honking of the cars behind her brought her back to reality.

She pulled over to the side of the road to gather her thoughts. And in her searching for direction from the Lord, she found herself turning around and retracing her path home. As she neared their house, the old anxiety returned. Quietly, she slipped out of the car and hesitantly walked to the back door. Peering through the screen before entering, she couldn't believe her eyes. George was on his knees, wet and sweaty, scrubbing the kitchen floor!

Unable to contain herself any longer, she rushed into the kitchen and knelt beside him in the water and soap suds. "George, I love you so much!"

That day George grew ten feet tall in Claire's eyes.

That day Claire saw what George was really like and how much he cared for her. Through a humble act of submission, George successfully communicated his love. In turn, he received the respect he desired from his wife. That day the power struggle that had plagued their marriage for years was permanently removed. They both won. But the victory did not come through acts of dominance. It came through *the power of submission*.

THE DOMINANCE/SUBMISSION STRUGGLE

Why has there been such a struggle over the principle of submission in marriage? The subject guarantees lively discussion whenever it is brought up in social gatherings, especially when a marriage counselor is one of the guests.

"Wives submit to your own husbands" is the phrase from Ephesians 5:22 that husbands too often hurl at their wives during the fight for control of the relationship. Somewhere we have acquired an erroneous notion that we must control every aspect of a relationship to be happy. For years men have been given the label of chauvinist, reflecting their attitude of superiority over females.

Then a backlash occurred as the women's movement retaliated with significant changes in our social patterns. In many cases these were welcome changes, especially in the workplace. But the concept of submission in the home continued to be viewed negatively.

As the institution of marriage made its way through these troubled waters of social change, the traditional husband/wife roles were discarded. Lack of role definition created new struggles with regard to who submits to whom. However, the fundamental principles of marriage based upon the authority of the Holy Scriptures remain unchanged, and those eternal principles must be followed to discover true intimacy and joy. Such is the case with submission within the marriage.

The problem usually starts with a false assumption that the counterpart of submission is dominance. If a wife is to be submissive to her husband (as the Bible says), then it should logically follow that he is to exercise dominance over her. But the Bible doesn't indicate that a husband should dominate his wife.

Confusion comes from our not fully understanding the place of submission in *all* of our lives. Understanding the power of submission is essential not only to your marriage but also to other relationships. Service offered in the spirit of submissiveness is the hallmark of Christian living. Jesus set the example: "For who is greater, he who sits at the table, or he who serves? Is it not he who sits at the table? Yet I am among you as the One who serves."[1]

TRUE SOURCE OF AUTHORITY

True authority springs from your service to, not your demand from, the people over whom you have authority. Placing the needs of the other person before your own may appear to be passive subjugation, but it is actually the key to healthy relationships and true authority.

We know that Christ had all authority to forgive sins and all other authority in heaven and on earth. Yet it was Jesus who gave repeated instruction by word and example of how authority was to be wielded. He condemned the ungodly concepts of authority and said the true way of leading is by serving.[2]

The teacher serves the student, the doctor serves the patient, and the pastor serves the parishioner. All discover authority within their respective roles. Look at those whose authority you respect. What is the basis for your respect? Respected authority is earned by serving.

Not only did Jesus tell His disciples that He was their servant but He also showed them. One vivid example was on the night of the Passover. He had broken the bread and served the cup. Then in the humblest way, similar to the lowliest of slaves, he knelt and washed the disciples' feet.

In our earlier story, George reflected Jesus' model of service by scrubbing the kitchen floor.

Jesus demonstrated His ultimate submission as He went to the cross to die for our sins. He died in a virtual garbage dump on the outskirts of Jerusalem, hanging on a cross between two convicted criminals:

> Therefore God also has highly exalted Him and given Him the name which is above every name, that at the name of Jesus every knee should bow, of those in heaven and those on earth and of those under the earth, and that every tongue should confess that Jesus Christ is Lord, to the glory of God the Father.[3]

SUBMISSION IN MARRIAGE

Take the principle of submissive service back into the marriage and examine the lesson from Ephesians 5. Many of us are familiar with the authority and order of responsibility in this passage.

Yet there is another powerful message on service and unity in Ephesians 5, which is often overlooked. Too often we immediately get off track by focusing our attention on verse 22, which states, "Wives, submit to your own husbands, as to the Lord."

Although it's tempting to concentrate on that verse, view the entire chapter in context. We are invited to be followers of God. One translation says we should be "imitators."[4] Therefore, our behavior should reflect a God-like stature.

First, we read a series of verses telling us how *not* to act. Look prayerfully at the list to determine which of these may apply to you. If some do apply, confess them and determine to remove them from your life.

The message then moves to a circumspectful walk with the Lord. We are told in verse 18 not to be drunk with wine, but to let our joy come from the filling of the Spirit in our lives. If we do allow the filling of the Spirit in our lives, unexpected things happen that are unusual to our human nature. Because of this supernatural joy, Paul and Silas sang to the Lord while trapped in prison.[5]

Next we find that, with the Spirit, we give thanks for *all* things—the good and the bad. Now we all know that it is natural to give thanks for good things. But the test of the Spirit's presence comes when you find yourself giving thanks for *all* things.

Another sign of the fullness of the Spirit is "submitting to one another in the fear of God" (verse 21). Realize that submission is unnatural behavior. Pride and self-centeredness, often identified as walking in the flesh, are natural without the Spirit. But when the Spirit controls our lives, certain supernatural things happen which change our nature. One of these is to become subject to one another out of reverence for Christ, which is part of being imitators of God.

Just as wives are submissive to husbands, we are to be submissive one to another. Now men, before you slip back into the old notion of domination, read on. Husbands are to love their wives as Christ loved the church (verse 25).

Look at that admonition. If you are having trouble openly showing your love to your wife, pause for a moment and focus on how you are loved by Christ. Think about it. He loved you first before you began to consider your response to Him. Initiate love toward your wife. Go first and start that loving process. In so doing you will be modeling a love similar to Christ's love for the church.

Second, the love you offer must be unconditional. If it's conditional, it isn't true love. John Powell, in his book *Unconditional Love,* wrote:

> There is no third possibility: love is either conditional or un-

> conditional. Either I attach conditions to my love for you or I do not. To the extent that I do attach such conditions, I do not really love you. I am only offering an exchange, not a gift. And true love is and must always be a free gift.[6]

Like any gift, the gift of Christ's love is not ours until we receive it. The same is true in the marital gift of love.

Third, the husband's gift of love must be sacrificial. This means he gives without primary regard for himself: "Husbands, love your wives, just as Christ also loved the church and *gave* Himself for it" (verse 25). When a husband loves his wife in this way, submission falls into its proper place, not as a command but as a *natural response to his love*. Then submissive service leads to unity.

By no means am I questioning the supreme authority and lordship of Christ in our lives. But careful reading of this chapter reflects an emphasis on *submissive service* leading to unity. This principle, as we have shown, is intricately woven into the principle of authority, which accompanies our God-given roles in marriage.

I once met with a young, talented couple. Each was carving an exciting career path. One was quickly moving up the ladder in the computer industry; the other was a junior partner in a local law firm. They had a terrific marriage, but they wanted advice about problems with one of their mothers.

During the session, the wife spoke up: "Honey, as long as we're at the marriage counselor's office, I want to make one thing distinctly clear. Don't ever expect me to fall into that submissive place where your dad expects your mom to be. We are equals in every respect."

Her husband was quick to respond, "Sweetheart, don't ever change! If you were anything but your aggressive, independent self, you would be someone I wouldn't know and probably wouldn't love."

Their banter was somewhat in jest, but both of them knew that if the husband exercised any form of dominant control he would have his hands full.

Near the end of the session, the husband turned to his wife and said, "I have a very full schedule today. Would you do a favor for me?"

"Honey, there is absolutely nothing I wouldn't do for you!" she said. At that moment I intentionally cleared my throat to get her attention. Need I say more? She realized what she had done. This aggressive, independent woman had placed herself in a submissive position to her husband. And it was as natural as can be. Why? Because submission is the natural response to love.

A LESSON IN UNITY

Marriage is intended to be the hallmark of unity between two individuals. Submissive service, mutually offered within the marriage, leads to a special oneness which the Scriptures describe as "one flesh."[7] To know this oneness requires a fuller understanding of the Greek work *kephale,* translated "head" in Ephesians 5:23: "For the husband is *head* of the wife, as also Christ is *head* of the church; and He is the Savior of the body."[8]

Whenever we ask who is head of a company, we are looking for the leader, the chief, the person in charge. Unfortunately, we have carried this contemporary connotation of the term *head*—one who is superior to or has authority over—into the marriage.[9] Yet the Greek word *kephale* used for head in Ephesians 5 applies more to the head/body metaphor. Christ is the head; the church is the body. The husband is the head; the wife is the body.

Whenever Paul, the author of this passage, used the metaphor of the human body in the Scriptures, he was teaching unity and mutual dependence of all parts on each other. This passage does not emphasize authority, but rather oneness and unity.[10]

Another meaning of *kephale* is "the source of life."[11] Applying this to the marital relationship, we could say the husband is "the source" of the wife as Christ is "the source" of the church.

Once woman and man were one in Adam. Man was the

source of woman as Eve was taken from Adam's rib.[12] Originally, there was one; then, there were two. In marriage the two once again become one.[13] Marriage is God's uniting two persons in one flesh. This unity reflects the love relationship above all love relationships, that between Christ and the Church.

Men frequently tend to miss another aspect of submission because they inaccurately regard submissiveness and weakness as synonymous. Men live by the myth that women are drawn to them primarily because of their strength, confidence, and independence, wrapped in the package called masculinity. But, in reality, that is only part of the truth.

In fact, women are often drawn to men because of their vulnerability, not their strength. Look at the plot of a good love story. Time after time the woman is attracted as she views the man's vulnerability. Her sense of being needed creates the powerful magnetism that draws them together.

All relationships are formed and maintained on meeting one another's needs. The greatest need we have is *the need to be needed*. Do you have the courage to let your partner know that he or she is needed in a deeply intimate way? At the risk of becoming vulnerable, let your needs be known. You will be opening the door to a new level of intimacy. Submission is not a sign of weakness. Submission is strength.

Chapter Fourteen

Fun Is Serious Business

Can *fun* actually have an important place in your marriage? You bet it can! Not only is fun important, but it is essential to the success of your marriage. When fun leaves your marriage, view it as an early sign of trouble. You must take action to change it.

This was the case of a conservative lady approaching middle age. She came for counsel with regard to some strange behavior her husband had demonstrated.

"My husband had intended to trade in our old station wagon for a more efficient second car that he could drive to work. You will never guess what he brought home in its place—a motorcycle! One of those big Harley Davidsons! I asked him what a middle-aged father of four thought he was doing with a dangerous machine like that? He never really answered me, but just rode off. What do you think this all means?" she inquired.

Before I could reply, she continued.

"Every evening he likes to go riding. When I complain, he seems to leave earlier and return later. I've got a problem, don't you think?"

"It all depends," I replied.

"Well, how many marriages do you know where husbands do strange things like this?" she asked.

My mind quickly went to my own marriage. We don't

ride motorcycles, but we do have mopeds, a sailboat, and a bright orange van which holds the key to some of our most treasured memories.

"What should I do?" she inquired with all sincerity.

"Do you have a pair of blue jeans?" I asked.

"Yes, but I only wear them when I work in the yard," she responded cautiously.

"Put them on tonight," I suggested, "and when your husband goes for his evening ride, jump on the back and go along."

"You must be kidding!" she blurted in shock.

Then she began to ponder the idea. She said she had wondered what made her husband enjoy riding. With a flavor of adventure in her voice she said, "I'll do it!"

Sometimes we search for a serious solution to our problems when a light touch is what we need. I was hoping that this would be the case with this woman. It seemed that what this couple really needed could be found *by sharing* what initially appeared to be the problem. And it could be fun.

Three weeks later she returned. Smiling with delight, she exclaimed that we had fixed their marriage in one session.

"I did what you said and had a babysitter lined up for after supper. As my husband went out to get on his motorcycle, he noticed the babysitter and asked where I was going. I said, 'With you!' And I jumped on the back of the motorcycle. He really seemed shocked, but the smile on his face told me he was pleased."

She said they had started riding together regularly. They had explored new areas and found a very private place where they shared a picnic supper. Then one evening something occurred that really cinched the newfound closeness in their marriage. "I told my husband that I couldn't ride with him that night. I needed to pack for two of our children who were leaving in the morning for summer Bible camp. Reluctantly, he rode off alone for the first time in over two weeks."

"What happened?" I asked.

"A few minutes later I heard him return, shut off the engine, and come into the kitchen. I asked him what was wrong. You know what he told me? 'It isn't fun anymore, without you.'"

Case closed.

What had initially appeared to be a problem that would have divided this couple became a "vehicle" that drew them closer together. We can learn several principles regarding the place of fun in solving marital problems.

First of all, fun is often a diversion from your routine. Do something different and new. Second, fun needs to be a shared experience where the pleasure is enjoyed by both partners. Take a second look at a particular activity that you never considered doing with your spouse. Initially, Judy never considered sailing a spirited M–16 sailboat. Today she is the best crew a skipper could ever want. Third, fun is based on the feelings the experience produces. An element of joy and happiness must be experienced and shared by both partners.

Our yard has always been a playground for the neighborhood children. One day in the midst of their play, I overheard one child say, "This is no fun! I'm going home." With that pronouncement, she promptly left the group. I thought *Typical kids!* recalling similar behavior in my own childhood. How often when we stopped having fun we promptly took our toys and went home.

During that same week I was visiting with a man who had recently left his long-term employment. When I asked what had prompted such a drastic step midpoint in his career, he replied, "My work simply wasn't fun anymore. I couldn't stand another day of it."

His honest response, along with the child's comment, taught me the serious implication the absence of fun has in the survival of a relationship. In one case the situation was *work* while the other was *play*. But the principle remains the same. *When fun leaves, relationships grow apart and often end.*

WHAT IS FUN?

What is this familiar yet elusive factor that so impacts our lives? The answer doesn't come easily. Something may be fun for one person but not for another. We have all been guests at a party when the hostess attempts to generate fun by announcing a new game. Everyone courteously attempts to enter in, but the good time just doesn't happen.

The key to fun lies not in the activity but in the *feelings* that result from the experience. This often requires an element of spontaneity.

Tim and Sally are a compulsive, tightly scheduled young couple. Beeping digital watches and pocket calendars control their lives. Seeing their need for some fun, I strongly urged them to take a break from this pattern by indulging in a "Pamper in Pink" weekend at a downtown hotel. Prompted only by my firm recommendation, they scheduled it on their calendars.

They had their weekend and it was successful. But nothing went as planned. To get the most out of their weekend, they had fully scheduled the time with dinner reservations, concert tickets, and a gallery tour. Sally had decided to get an early start by sneaking downtown midafternoon to prepare for the evening at the hotel. Her husband had taken their suitcase in his car that morning. Sally arrived in a taxi with only her overnight case and her guitar to serenade her husband. Wearing jeans and a sweatshirt with her hair in rollers, she slipped into the hotel to quickly check in. And then the problems began.

Inadvertently, she had left her purse in the taxi, so she was without money or identification. Her husband was out of the office and could not be reached. Her only alternative was to settle into an inconspicuous corner of the lobby to wait.

Hours passed before her distinguished husband arrived in a dark pin-striped suit. Glancing across the lobby, he saw his embarrassed wife in a corner of the sofa. Being shy, both had very little to say as they walked to the elevator. It seemed as if everyone in the lobby was staring at them. Furthermore, Sally knew she was going to be late for dinner because they were already behind schedule.

Arriving at their suite, they closed the door and just stared at each other. Realizing she was hungry, Sally impulsively dove into the basket of fruit on the dresser. Tim laughed as he watched her sit in the middle of the giant heart-shaped bed and stuff herself with fruit. He loosened his tie and joined her.

Next, she provided an impromptu concert on her guitar. Then, while she soaked in a bubble bath, he sang ballads, slightly off-key. They forgot their gourmet dinner, and savored hot onion soup and french bread at a nearby cafe instead. They also missed the concert at Orchestra Hall but created their own in their room at the hotel.

As you can see, nothing went as anticipated but they discovered the joy of spontaneity. The weekend had been different. It had truly been fun.

FUN CAN UNLOCK INTIMACY

Couples who have lost intimacy in their relationship can often be heard making some of the following comments:

"We never laugh anymore."
"I don't think she even knows how to have fun."
"He just isn't any fun to be with."
"We are too old to have fun like that."

Fun is often a missing ingredient for couples in marital trouble. Conversely, as a relationship is being restored, fun returns to the couples' lives. Can you answer the following questions?

Do you have fun with your spouse?
If not, what blocks it?
What creates fun for you with your partner?

When fun is absent, you grow apart. Conversely, when you are emotionally distant from your spouse, fun can be the key that unlocks the door to newfound intimacy. Such was the case with Jack and Carla.

Jack and Carla had been attending group therapy sessions with no apparent progress. Part of their block was because Carla had been involved in an affair several months earlier.

She knew she needed to share this with Jack. But so far, the element of safety in the relationship had not presented an open door.

One night after an extremely tense group session, Jack and Carla decided not to go directly home. Searching for something novel to relieve the tension, they wandered into a theatre just in time to catch the beginning of a comedy. The film did its job and started their laughter.

Relaxed and entertained after leaving the theater, they stopped for a large pizza. Now they were more ready to return home. The relief of the transformed evening accompanied them. Jack made a quip about group therapy, which ignited more laughter to the point of tears. Neither could stop.

Suddenly, the interaction took a new turn. Like a dam bursting, the words, feelings, fears, and events all flowed together as Carla poured out her secret. The tears continued, but they were no longer the product of laughter. Instead, they reflected the deep sadness of her heart. Jack and Carla had reached a new level of intimacy in their marriage. Trust and commitment were being tested. The risks were high.

Jack pulled the car off to the side of the road. He paid full attention to Carla. Asking for his forgiveness, Jack's response took Carla by surprise. He not only forgave her but also asked forgiveness for his evident neglect in their marriage. That evening the healing process truly began in their lives.

The key element that broke the logjam was not confrontation, deep insight, or some other sophisticated psychological process. It was their experience of fun. In the midst of tension, fun performed a serious function, removing barriers and leaving an openness for the intimate conversation that followed.

Fun removes defensive walls. Humor and laughter become vehicles for serious, productive communication. It is this spontaneous part of us, ignited by fun, that is most apt to reveal our intimate side. Determine to make fun an integral part of your marriage.

KEY ESSENTIALS FOR FUN

1. The experience must be fully enjoyed by both.
2. Active participation produces more fun for the couple than their spectating.
3. Fun should not be overly planned. Let spontaneity do its work.
4. Fun must be a diversion from your disciplined routine.

Fun does not abandon discipline but, instead, underscores it by its contrasting diversion. As a result, fun introduces contrasts. A walk in the woods is fun after sitting behind a desk all day. However, to sit on your patio is fun after being on your feet for hours doing yard work. Just as a mountain is not recognized without the valley, so is the presence of fun not realized without discipline.

As we saw with Tim and Sally, the element that produced fun was the spontaneity of diversion from their usual demanding schedules. As we read earlier in the book, the notion of an evening free just to have fun creates guilt for many Christian couples. This negative emotion quickly extinguishes any hope for joy and happiness that might result from such an experience. Don't get caught in this trap. Allow fun to have its place in your marriage as a major element to your intimacy and well-being.

Chapter Fifteen

Security for Your Marriage

Go back with me to that time when you and your spouse first met and started dating. As you fell in love and the relationship moved closer toward marriage, remember how everyone seemed to get into the act? Especially if your chosen partner met everyone's approval? Friends, parents, relatives, church members, and anyone else around rushed to give their support and encouragement to the budding new lovers.

"Aren't they a cute couple? They seem to be so much in love," people whispered behind your backs (but loudly enough so you would be sure to hear). The support intensified as the wedding day became more of a reality. Everyone smiled and gave their nods of approval as you walked by.

Whenever Mom went shopping she purchased two of whatever was on sale. After all, she knew "the kids" could use one to set up housekeeping. Showers were given. Plans were made. The one hundred and one details that required attention were efficiently cared for by the massive team of people who automatically seemed to come together to pull this whole thing off. At that time it seemed as if the whole world revolved around these two who would be married soon. Absolutely nothing could interfere with the activities involved in planning the wedding. They came first.

The security was great. There was really nothing to worry

about because someone else was taking care of everything. If some task did happen to fall on your shoulders, you had plenty of help from others. No one turned you down, whatever the request might have been. Friends and family were all around you. They needed to be a part of your wedding. Nothing bad could happen. You were in secure hands and it felt good.

No one could have received more encouragement from friends and family than Judy and I had. The fact that her father had been the pastor of our church automatically gave us an edge on receiving support from the entire congregation. Six weeks prior to our wedding, he died unexpectedly. This generated additional support from everyone around. People cared and they showed it. They could not seem to do enough for us.

Even Judy's boss quietly pressed a wadded bill into the palm of my hand during a handshake. It was obvious to me that he didn't want Judy or any of the others standing around to know what he had done. "Have an evening out on me," he whispered. Later, when I unwrapped the bill and saw that it was a twenty, I knew we would have at least two nights out (remember, it was 1960) with some left over.

All this support and security continued to build to that exciting climax, the wedding.

Although we didn't realize it at the time, the wedding was a beginning for us but a culmination for everyone else. They had accomplished their mission and now could return to their day-to-day routine. Life would go on as usual for everyone but us, the newlyweds.

We were in for the shock of our lives. The realization of being on our own had not yet hit us. Riding high on the enthusiasm of the celebration of our wedding night, we left on our honeymoon.

A dramatic emptiness hit us as we returned. Ten days earlier we had left a church and a parsonage filled with food, flowers, laughter, and the gaiety of happy people celebrating our wedding. The memory of that night had continued throughout our honeymoon.

Now, tired from our trip yet excited over the anticipation of being home, we pulled in late at the parsonage. Both of us looked for the evidence of someone awaiting our return, but the house was dark and void of any signs of life. That was strange for the church parsonage. Speechless, we sat for a moment in our car just staring at the house. It had never looked so desolate to either of us.

Slowly we got out and walked in the back door. Although the house was dark, the silence was even worse. Our only greeting was a brief note taped to the opened door of an unplugged refrigerator. It told us that Judy's mother had gone to look for a house in the city where she would be moving. As we looked around, things were already packed in boxes ready for shipping. Although it had once been home, we now felt like we were walking into someone else's house.

Flopping a mattress over on the floor, we made a makeshift bed and comforted ourselves by the fact that tomorrow things would be better. We would drive on to my parents' home to celebrate the Fourth of July in a manner that has been tradition for as long as I can remember.

Morning came quickly and we could not seem to get out of that house soon enough. It was no longer home. As we drove away we saw the house merely as a place of memories. Our wedding day, ten days earlier, seemed like ancient history.

Needing to reclaim some of that enthusiasm and interest we had enjoyed so much before our wedding, I drove as fast as I could to my little hometown of Lyle. Even the short ten-mile trip over familiar roads to this little farming community seemed to take longer than usual. But a sense of happiness returned, and we felt excitement in the air as we pulled into the town getting ready for its celebration of the year.

At first the realization didn't hit us that the jubilation had nothing to do with our return. Our time had been two weeks earlier when we were married. That was past, and now the attention was on other things. Oh yes, everyone was moving about with a similar excitement and dedication. But this time it was for the parade on Main Street. My father happened to be in charge of it that year. Then there was the traditional picnic that was served on the front porch following the morning festivities. Everyone was busy, and this time we were in the way.

All the support and interest from our Christian community that had given us such a sense of security had somehow vanished. Before our wedding we had been the center of attention; now we seemed almost transparent as people walked by us. Sensing abandonment, we silently thought to ourselves, *Where will we turn for our security?*

THE CHURCH AT A SAFE DISTANCE

In one way or another this question is asked by almost every newlywed couple as they move from singleness into marriage. In contrast to the abundant support and interest generously given by the church prior to the wedding, the absence of response in the months that follow is a distinct letdown. Just when the new husband and wife seem to need this sustenance the most, they receive it the least. It is wrong to assume that the church is doing them a favor by leaving them alone. They need that continued acceptance and support as they adjust to being married.

Another time when the church seems to maintain a "safe" distance from its married couples is when they appear to be having problems. The church often takes the stance that it is none of their business, that they should not interfere. Actually, the opposite is true. This is the time when the church should step in to perform its function of looking after the needs of *all* its members.

One Christian woman, whose husband became involved with another woman and ultimately left home, told me, "Living in the evangelical subculture produced certain standards of behavior and pressures that proscribed my wanting to be open with our problems. It was not spiritual to have a problem marriage. Since Fred and I were committed Christians and had chosen to serve God, I guess I thought the problems would magically disappear."

Then she went on to give some incredibly significant advice to Christians with rocky marriages: "I'd help them realize that if they are having problems, they need the help and encouragement of the body of Christ. It's not likely they'll make it alone."

Notice how the apostle Paul instructs the early church:

> There should be no schism in the body, but . . . the members should have the same care for one another. And if one member suffers, all the members suffer with it, or if one member is honored, all the members rejoice with it. Now you are the body of Christ, and members individually.[1]

As a husband and wife turn to each other to build or rebuild their marriage, they will realize that they must have support from outside their relationship. Their isolation must be broken. As one authority tells us, "It is simply not sensible to ask two people, usually young and inexperienced, to assume important and complex responsibilities without any resources or support. The family never before operated in splendid isolation, and in a time of great confusion it is even more vulnerable."[2]

Poets and sociologists tell us that no man is an island. Neither are marriages. As a husband and wife need each other, they also need a base of support outside of themselves whereby they can receive guidance, support, and a sense of belonging. For the evangelical Christian, this community or base must be the local church. The marriage must identify with and draw on that body of believers who are committed to one another and are living under the divine authority of God as He instituted it through His church.

Throughout this book sometimes I have been hard on the church because I believe someone needs to say, "Back off and let people have some time at home." Please don't interpret this criticism to mean I believe the church is obsolete or unable to fulfill its ancient purpose of caring not only for individual believers but also for marriages.

The purpose of the church remains unchanged. Its power is still there. The problem is that the church has become silent. Passiveness toward troubled Christian marriages reflects neglect of the authority given to the church by God to shepherd marriages and families.

Sermons and seminars on marriage and family life are routinely included in church programs. I have had the privilege of being a part of several in churches in our area. But seminars are not enough. The church must go further. It must sense the responsibility to look after each marriage within its group of believers. If a marriage is left to its own support and control and it falters, there is no other place to turn.

Even back in the Old Testament the problems of marriages did not go unchecked or undisciplined. God simply did not let things go by the board. He instituted a government called Israel to look after the care and discipline of His people.

Similarly, in the New Testament the Lord established a government here on earth through which His grace could be fostered, His discipline carried out, His care exhibited, and His love made real. That government is present in His church. The place where marriages grow must be in the garden called the church.

In 1 Corinthians, Paul gave explicit instructions on how the church should care not only for people who had been divorced, widowed, or single, but also for married people. The time has come to reinstate in the church the same kind of care and commitment for its members that was present when *Israel* walked with God and when the *church* walked with God.

RESPONSIBLE TO CARE

I have learned that, in different places around the country, some churches are regaining their vision to care for marriages. In one church it became apparent to everyone that a husband and wife were growing distant with one another. Two of the church elders got together with them and gently told them that several in the church had noticed that their marriage had outwardly eroded. The way they had appeared for weeks in the services and elsewhere had caused grave concern that their marriage was in difficulty.

They readily admitted their problems to these two men who, as leaders in the church, had approached them with love and concern. (Contrary to what you may expect, I have learned from experience as a group therapist that direct confrontation coupled with love and honest concern will almost always bring a positive response from the couple. Remember, people want to be open if they know it is safe. In this situation the directness of the elders opened the door.)

These men continued to work with the couple, rebuilding their confidence in the love of their relationship. The elders told them that if they were needed day or night, they were just a phone call away. The couple knew they meant it. They made progress and the direction of their marriage took a complete turnabout. Remember, you can lovingly confront a couple when you are committed to stay by them as long as they need you.

When the leadership in the church takes responsibility or appoints someone in the membership to look after a troubled marriage within their fellowship, amazing things happen. Not too long ago the deacons at a church asked a happily married couple to look after a husband and wife whose marriage was in difficulty. The appointed couple was instructed to sit and listen to the other couple once a week, trusting that through God's leading they would be given wisdom from the Lord to say and do things to enable the marriage to straighten out. Benefits are often realized by both couples as they go through an experience such as this. Several weeks later, it became evident that the Lord used this weekly session to put the troubled marriage back on the right track.

People caring for people is necessary to heal relationships. Consistently, the couples I see in group therapy do better than those who come in alone for office sessions. I believe the primary difference is that the presence of others gives care and support. A husband and wife will become strong as they draw from a base outside of their marriage. For the evangelical Christian, this base is the church.

I believe educational programs for marriages and families should continue. Seminars on family life are an important part of the church program and reflect a positive, healthy trend. But don't be deluded into believing that the discipleship of marriages ends there. That is just skimming the surface. The church's responsibility includes discipline and authoritative correction as well as love and nurture.

How to do it is the next issue. In any relationship, something must be done from both sides. The solution requires consistent, sincere effort. It is not easy, but it can be done.

Let me speak first to the married couple. Whether or not you are having problems, plug in quickly to your church. Attend the services and fellowship with the members. Don't wait for them to reach out to you. Reach out to them.

If you are sensing problems in your marriage, I urge you to drop the pride that has kept you from being open with others about it. After praying about your situation, go to your church leadership with your need. Trust your pastor, deacon, or elder with your problems. God will, in turn, use the church to meet your needs. This is His plan. In obedience to Him, turn to your church for help.

To the church leadership, let me urge you to become bold again with the authority given you by God to guide the marriages of your local church membership. Become actively involved in the care and guidance you are instructed by God to give as part of your function in the church body. You may do this personally or you may feel led to instruct another couple to help out with a troubled marriage.

If you sense that a couple is having problems and they do not come to you, go to them! It is your responsibility. This may mean putting yourself in an uncomfortable situation from time to time, but when it is done with love and the guidance of God people will thank you. In most cases God will work through you to save a marriage and family. Remember that these couples are part of your church family, and what you are doing *is* part of the function of the church.

The church's neglect in this area has created silence in response to cries for help by evangelical marriages. Maybe our ears have been deaf to the cry. But now *listen* and you will *hear*. As you hear the cries for help, reach out in boldness, claiming the power given to you by God through His Holy Spirit. As the shepherd left the ninety-nine for the moment to go after the one lost sheep, let the church take the time and make the effort to reach out to the one lost marriage, rescuing it from destruction and divorce. Let us remain silent no longer.

Chapter Sixteen

The Plus Element

Throughout this book we have looked at marriages. We have explored what they are and what they can become. As you look around, two visible extremes stand out: good marriages and bad ones. But many are just average—neither good nor bad. They just go on day after day. You see them, but there is nothing that stands out as special. They are just together.

Like your Christian walk, marriage was designed by God to be a beautiful, exciting experience that grows throughout your entire lifetime. Unfortunately, for many this never happens. Some marriages fail and end in divorce. Others fail but continue to exist legally.

Failing marriages are becoming more visible among Christians. We see increasing numbers getting divorced. There is also that silent group who remain married but endure an empty, frustrating, and unfulfilling relationship.

Are you in either of these groups? If you are like others I know, you watch the good marriages closely, secretly hoping to get some clues on how to make your marriage better. Looking over the masses of couples, every now and then you see one with something special in their relationship. You envy it but can't seem to identify what it is. It has to do with the way they look at each other and the way they touch. A special awareness of each other seems to be present.

I believe these couples have discovered the uniqueness of the marriage relationship. They know and experience the fulfillment God intended for their union when He created it. Their marriages possess what I call the "plus element." This element is something extra that lifts their relationship above the mediocrity of the masses. Even though in today's society it is a rarity, in the beginning it was God's plan that all marriages have this quality.

As the plus element becomes a part of your marriage, you will notice some changes in both you and your marriage. There will be a sense of oneness, and you won't be able to conceive of being single again. As a matter of fact, you will have difficulty recalling that time in your life when you were alone. Singleness as you previously experienced it will become foreign to you.

Often Judy will ask if I was having a rough time at a given hour of that day. When I discuss it with her, she inevitably replies that she felt it too, and sensed the need to pray for me then. Daily, you are intensely aware of your partner even though you are apart. Indeed, you are never alone.

SEVEN KEYS TO DEVELOP THE PLUS ELEMENT IN YOUR MARRIAGE

Carefully studying our marriage, as well as others who seem to have the plus element, I have discovered certain keys that can help you develop it in your marriage. Follow these seven keys and you will also begin to experience the warm, fulfilling marriage God designed for you.

1. RELATIONSHIPS

The first key in establishing the plus element is to recognize that your marriage is a relationship. Furthermore, it is the most important relationship God has given to all married couples. Therefore, all the rules we have discussed for forming and maintaining relationships especially apply here. Your marriage deserves your very best nurture and care. In return, it will grow strong and not fail.

You are an important part of your marriage but not all of

it. What is done and experienced by one affects the other. Both of you share your successes, likewise, both share your failures. You are together.

At the time you said your wedding vows God tied the knot creating your relationship and lifted it above you as an individual. *From then on the relationship was to come before yourself.* It is something bigger than you alone.

2. *GIVING*

Focus on giving, and receiving will come automatically. When you are preoccupied with receiving from your partner, the result is a competitiveness that will break down the marriage. Giving is tangible evidence of your love. Giving and loving go hand in hand. One feeds the other.

Find a need and experience the joy of meeting it, expecting nothing in return. Oh, you will receive; but it will come as a natural response to your giving.

One afternoon I was scooping some ice cubes out of the freezer in the kitchen at our clinic to take home to make homemade ice cream. Our son, Peter, had just spent all his babysitting money to purchase an electric ice cream maker for the family. We were excited about trying it for the first time. (Actually, we had a hand-operated freezer in storage that we hadn't used for years because we were too lazy to turn the crank for forty-five minutes to an hour.)

While in the kitchen, I struck up a conversation with our cook. She told me she had been looking all over for a hand-operated freezer but could not find one. She explained that she needed one with a hand crank because she has nine grandchildren and for them the fun of making ice cream was for each to get a turn at the crank.

"I have one!" I told her.

"You do?" she replied, her eyes lighting up. "How much do you want for it?" she asked.

"I'll talk it over with my wife and let you know," I replied.

After returning to my office, I telephoned Judy and said, "I've got a buyer for our old ice-cream freezer. How much shall we ask for it?"

After I explained who was interested in buying it, Judy came up with the perfect price. "Let's give it to her," she suggested.

We did, and I have heard many times how much she and her grandchildren have enjoyed homemade ice cream. Since then we constantly have been receiving corn, tomatoes, and other beautiful vegetables from her garden. Priced in the grocery store, the vegetables far exceeded the value of both the old and new freezer combined. I just wish I could find something else to give her!

This is a simple illustration of a truth that repeats itself, and it works best in your marriage. Giving is love made visible. When you are faced with tension and problems in your marriage, try giving. If you will give unconditionally and long enough, your partner will respond. The tension will leave, and the problem will be solved or just go away. God has promised it.

3. ADJUSTMENTS

The marriage relationship is dynamic. It is constantly changing. Recognize that there will always be highs and lows and they are normal. The presence of highs and lows is not bad. *Expect* them. The important thing is for you to be able to *adjust* to them. The dynamics of adjusting to challenges and stresses reflect that your marriage is vibrant and alive. Your ability to adjust becomes a way of life and a key to the success of your marriage.

4. COMMUNICATION

Always keep communicating. Daily let your spouse know your thoughts, feelings, needs, and expectations. Realize that communication is a skill that requires constant practice. It must be maintained and can always be improved. Most of all, remember that communication is the pipeline, and what is said is the food that feeds your marriage relationship. If the pipeline is blocked and communication stops, the relationship will eventually starve and die. Through full and rich communication, the relationship will be nourished and will continue to grow strong and vibrant.

5. SPONTANEITY

In the marriage relationship there must be a time for impulsiveness, a time when your behavior is free from logic. Spontaneity encourages you and your spouse to do something simply because you feel like it. When your marriage is filled with daily controls and responsibilities, an occasional moment when you give in to your impulsiveness together is like a breath of fresh air after being in a stuffy room.

I will never forget a certain Saturday afternoon when our children were younger. My wife and I seldom got out of the house together. There were several reasons, but the main one was that we couldn't afford babysitters. This afternoon we felt we did not have a choice. We had to go a wedding. We didn't know the couple well, but we were friends of the groom's parents. So we made the supreme sacrifice and hired a babysitter.

We parked the car, entered the church, and took our place in line waiting restlessly to sign the guest book. Judy and I looked at each other. We could read the other's mind without saying a word.

With a mischievous smile on my face I asked her, "Are you thinking what I am?"

She nodded, "Yes."

"You sign the guest book and I'll get the car," I said without a moment's hesitation. We missed the wedding but had one of the best afternoons of our lives.

Periodically, marriage needs that breath of fresh air. Do something unplanned. Let go of logic and go with your feelings. Just be sure to do it together!

6. TIME

Relationships are built on shared experiences, and experiences require time. There is nothing that can replace your spending time together in your marriage. No gifts, favors, or anything can take the place of you.

As you spend time together, *create traditions*. Traditions are those times you spend together in some way that are uniquely yours. This will become especially significant as children become a part of your home. They will enter in and help create the tradition. No one really knows exactly how traditions start, but once you have one nothing can change it. It is done that way year after year. (By the way, this creates a sense of security for everyone.)

One of our family's traditions takes place when we celebrate birthdays. We have discovered the joy of creating our own birthday cards. Peter, our oldest son, has always had an interest in drawing. In his typical grandiose fashion, he once made a large poster birthday card for his mother that covered the entire refrigerator door. Stephen, his younger brother, looking for the easiest way out, added his own greeting with a note and sketch on an empty corner of Peter's creation. Finally, Leah, our daughter, and I followed suit by joining in with our notes. This was the beginning of the family-birthday-card-on-the-refrigerator-door tradition. It now highlights each of our birthdays. The poster card gets photographed in colored prints and home movies. Our albums are filled with them. It remains on the refrigerator door for at least a week; no one dares discard it!

A tradition is important not for the activity itself, but for the importance it signifies in the relationship. It is a special time when people feel they truly belong to each other.

7. CHRIST-CENTEREDNESS

Center your marriage in Christ by committing your relationship to Him. Your marriage became an entity in itself when you were joined together. As you have committed your life to the Lord Jesus, do the same with your marriage. Together make the same commitment you did individually when you invited Christ to be Lord and Savior of your life. Turn your marriage over to Him and allow Him to protect and guide it. Once you have done so, daily acknowledge His presence through thanksgiving and prayer together. Remember, marriage is a model of our relationship with Christ.[1]

These are the seven keys to a warm, fulfilling marriage. Perhaps there could be more, or maybe different terms. But whether you like the terms or not, please remember the truths they represent. That is what is important. If these keys become a part of your marriage, not only will the quality of the relationship grow, but it also will be guaranteed to be permanent. The possibility of divorce will be inconceivable.

Do you remember when you were little and your shoes were always coming untied? Your mother probably taught you how to tie a double knot. This took just a little more effort and time than tying a single knot. Yet one thing was sure: It wouldn't come untied.

There is another advantage in a double knot. Can you remember one of your friends pulling on one strand of your shoelace? A single knot easily came untied. This was disturbing to me, especially before I had learned to tie my own shoelaces. One day my friend tried his usual stunt, but this time I had a double knot. Not only did the lace stay tied, but the knot became tighter.

Follow these seven keys of the plus element, and you will tie a double knot in your marriage. Then, not only will it stay tied, but also if someone tries to untie it, your marriage relationship will respond by drawing more tightly together. May you and your spouse discover this permanent, beautiful relationship with each other.

Chapter Seventeen

Will It Ever Be Like It Was?

There was warmth and happiness in their voices as they told me about the first years of their marriage. Those were good years. Everything had gone well and they had a great marriage. Their voices trailed off as their minds drifted silently to the way they were. I chose not to interrupt the silence and break the spell of happiness they were privately enjoying as they relived the past.

Suddenly, the stillness was broken, though there were no words. Her eyes started talking to me. They searched deeply into mine, looking for the answer first to see if the question should be asked. There was fear in her eyes. By now her husband had joined her. They were both thinking the same thought, even though neither spoke. Then the question had to be asked, "Will it ever be like it was?"

For those couples whose marriages once were good, yet now are in trouble, this question is always asked. They want some guarantee that the good they once experienced can be recaptured. Behind this question is the unspoken plea, *Reassure us that there is some possibility that our marriage will eventually get better.*

As you have gone with me through this book and related it to your marriage, perhaps you are asking the same question. By now you have started to become acquainted with me. You know a little about how I think and feel. You have sat with me in the office, visited the college classroom, and looked in on my marriage.

I have not had the same opportunity with you, nor should I. I haven't been able to read your eyes or hear your words, but your spouse has. Therefore, take what I have shared with you and turn to each other for your answers. Find them within the privacy and the intimacy of your own marriage.

"Will it ever be like it was?" My answer for you is one that has been given to me from couples I have known, couples who have worked out their problems and rebuilt their marriages. "No, it will not be the same; but it can be better." You can never return to a stage in your relationship from the past. You must always go on.

But if you are having problems, it does not mean it will always be that way. You will find that your marriage can become better than it was. But you must honestly commit yourselves to each other and work on it or it will not happen.

The problems we all encounter cause us to take an honest look at our marriage and make the changes necessary to improve them. We have grown in our relationships through commitment, communication, adjustment, and love. Often it occurred in that order. Now that you are aware of what it takes to build a good marriage, most of you can grow together before you have problems.

Several couples have told me, "I would never want to go though this again. Yet when I see where we are now, I am glad it happened. I would never go back to the 'glory days' of our past. Our relationship now is better than ever. But we had to pay a price to get here."

"Will it ever be like it was?" Go to your partner, the one you married, find the answer, and have the greatest time of your life!

How Can We Keep Christian Marriages from Falling Apart?

STUDY GUIDE

INTRODUCTION

In the learning process, what you hear you tend to forget. What you hear and see you tend to remember. But what you hear, see, and *do* becomes a part of you. This study guide offers an opportunity to apply what you have just read to your own marriage.

Use the discussion questions as guides to communicate privately with your spouse and also in discussion groups. The application exercises are varied and should be chosen selectively, depending upon your own marital needs and interests.

You will notice that the study guide is designed primarily for couples to use individually and with each other. However, it can also serve as a guide for discussion groups. If you plan to meet as a group, the size should not exceed five couples in order to experience effective interaction.

Confidentiality must be respected within the group to allow for greater trust and freedom. We all know that experience is a major source for learning. Therefore, the shared experiences of couples within a group can greatly enhance understanding and application of this book's subject matter.

Whether you utilize the study guide privately or in a group setting, it is my sincere desire and prayer that the principles and concepts set forth in this book will become a part of your personal experience.

SESSION 1

Review chapters 1, 2, and 3.

CONTENT SUMMARY

These three chapters deal with the principle that divorce is not a solution but rather an exchange of problems. What troubled couples believe can be found outside of their marriage can actually best be found within their marriage. The key lies in their commitment as stated in their wedding vows.

GOAL

To see more clearly the negative side of divorce and renew your commitment by reviewing the marriage vows.

QUESTIONS FOR DISCUSSION

1. What were Mark's feelings when Donna wanted to "try again"? Discuss similar feelings you may have experienced in your marriage.
2. Why is it an accurate comparison to equate divorce with death?
3. List Elizabeth Kübler-Ross's five phases of loss in dying. Discuss how these same emotions of loss can apply to the dissolution of a marriage.
4. In the vows "to love and to cherish" what is unique about the promise *to cherish?* Discuss ways in which you cherish your spouse.
5. Compare the phrase "so long as you both shall live" with "so long as you both shall love." What makes these vows different?

APPLICATION EXERCISE FOR MARRIAGE

1. List problems that can be solved by divorce. Next list the problems that are acquired by divorce. Compare and contrast the list.
2. Go back to the place where you proposed, or somewhere local that *reminds* you of that special place. Recall your courtship and renew your vows. Use chapter 3 from the book if you need help.

SESSION 2

Review chapters 4 and 5.

CONTENT SUMMARY

These two chapters focus on the importance of relationships in our lives and the unique role that the marriage relationship plays. Emphasis is on intimacy as the product of openness, revealing both the good and the bad, the pleasant and the unpleasant sides of ourselves to our spouse.

GOAL

To help you become more aware of the need-meeting process that is an essential part of your marital relationship.

QUESTIONS FOR DISCUSSION

1. The client, in the opening of chapter 4, needed answers to two basic questions about himself. What were they? Have you personally searched for answers to the same questions?
2. What are two basic emotional needs listed by Dr. Glasser in chapter 4? Examine and discuss how these needs are or are not being met in your own life.
3. Relationships are formed and maintained on a *mutual need-meeting activity*. Identify a time of tension in your marriage and determine if the need-meeting process was out of balance.
4. One of the greatest fears in relationships is the fear of rejection. Discuss a time when you experienced rejection and how it affected you.
5. Behavior and feelings are closely related in marriage. Discuss how one affects the other in your marriage. Which take priority in your life?

APPLICATION EXERCISE FOR MARRIAGE

1. List all your answers to the question, Who am I? Then do the same for the question, What am I like? Discuss your answers with your spouse or your group. Identify the relationships which have contributed to your answers.
2. Tell your spouse one trait within yourself that you believe is undesirable and that you would like to change. Allow your spouse the opportunity to suggest ways in which he or she can help you make this change. Analyze how you felt during this conversation.

SESSION 3

Review chapter 6.

CONTENT SUMMARY

This chapter shows that you can be close to your spouse at one time and later grow apart to the point that you are strangers. Growth apart often begins with a couple's neglecting their marriage because of outside demands and distractions. The marriage is set aside as other outside sources begin to take priority in meeting their needs. To protect against this happening in your marriage, your commitment must remain strong with a willingness to adjust to your partner's needs.

GOAL

To help you identify the signposts of becoming strangers again in your marriage and know the steps to take to keep it from happening.

QUESTIONS FOR DISCUSSION

1. Identify in your marriage those factors that can keep you from having your personal needs met.
2. What alternatives distract spouses from their marriage to have their personal needs of being loved and worthwhile met elsewhere?
3. Examine what you mean by commitment and identify ways to communicate this to your spouse.
4. What are some of your needs that should be met primarily in your marriage?
5. Identify the difference between being *willing* to adjust and being *able* to adjust. Give an example of each.

APPLICATION EXERCISE FOR MARRIAGE

Recall the time when you first met and were introduced to your spouse. You were total strangers to each other. Discuss those early perceptions with each other. Now, go on a date with your spouse and pretend you have just met. Share things about yourself you would want this person to know as you get better acquainted. Have the items that you consider important changed from when you first met?

SESSION 4

Review chapter 7.

CONTENT SUMMARY

The loss of romantic attraction is the subject of this chapter. While the initial attraction of infatuation diminishes, it can be replaced by a deeper more lasting marital passion. This is the product of a maturing marriage with the key elements identified by an Intimacy Ladder.

GOAL

To guide you in building greater intimacy within your marriage by applying the principles of the Intimacy Ladder.

QUESTIONS FOR DISCUSSION

1. How can you protect yourself from the experience of an unexpected attraction, such as Karen had at the class reunion?
2. Discuss the risks of experiencing passion prematurely, before the relationship has fully developed.
3. Explore the role of *harmony* when you feel close to your spouse.
4. List the five levels of the Intimacy Ladder and apply them to your marriage.
5. Identify the times when you sense the greatest atmosphere of safety within your marriage. What causes you to feel especially safe?

APPLICATION EXERCISE FOR MARRIAGE

1. Practice each of the levels of the Intimacy Ladder, beginning with *listening*. Identify a time when you have experienced each level within your marriage.
2. Read together Genesis 2:24. Talk about what you leave in addition to your mother and father to cleave to each other. In addition to the sexual union, identify areas in which you and your spouse sense a oneness reflecting the spirit of *one flesh*.

SESSION 5

Review chapter 8.

CONTENT SUMMARY

Your ability to communicate is key to the emotional feeding of your marriage. Communication fails when a message is not accurately or totally received. This chapter identifies the more common forms of communication failure and how to correct them.

GOAL

To be able to communicate meaningfully with your spouse.

QUESTIONS FOR DISCUSSION

1. The communication definition includes *thoughts, feelings,* and *expectations*. Identify an example of each in your marital communication.
2. List all the different methods you use to send a message, and give an example of each.
3. What are three methods of listening? Give an example of each in your communication with your spouse.
4. What are the five syndromes of communication breakdown? Discuss how these syndromes have affected communication with your spouse.
5. Identify three common methods of selective inattention. Which of these occur in your marriage?

APPLICATION EXERCISE FOR MARRIAGE

Mirroring Exercise

The following exercise teaches you how to improve your listening skills and creates a structure for better communication. It is especially useful when you are tempted to argue. Let me show you how to avoid arguing by practicing the technique of *mirroring*. I encourage you to give it a try.

1. Sit on two chairs facing each other, knee to knee, holding hands. Establish and maintain eye contact.
2. Begin by talking about a subject you have selected with your spouse. Your spouse does not interrupt but listens carefully in silence. Try to keep your message on one subject and be brief. When you have finished, inform your partner by saying that you are done.

3. Now your spouse replies, saying in his/her own words *what he/she heard you say*. The response must not include a personal reaction or effort to correct your message. These factors are sure to create a defensiveness that blocks communication. Your spouse must repeat only *what he or she heard you say*.

4. If the message is incorrect or your spouse misses a portion, repeat that part. Once you are satisfied with your spouse's response, you have completed half of the exercise.

5. Now reverse the process, allowing your spouse the same opportunity to give his/her message. Listen in silence. When your spouse is finished, repeat in your own words the message you heard. In similar fashion, your spouse has opportunity to correct any part of your response until you have repeated the full message.

6. The final step is to talk about the process you just experienced. Avoid further discussion of the subject which was presented. Focus on areas such as:

- how difficult or easy it was to listen
- how it felt to touch and have eye contact during the entire exercise
- the freedom of speaking, knowing that you would not be interrupted

SESSION 6

Review chapters 9 and 10.

CONTENT SUMMARY

These two chapters show the hazards of marriages in which partners are overly involved in the fulfilling of outside demands on their time and energy. Romantic experiences do not occur unless you make them happen. This often occurs only at the expense of other duties. It becomes a matter of priority.

GOAL

To help you budget your time so that you have quality experiences together in your marriage.

QUESTIONS FOR DISCUSSION

1. What was the author's response to his wife's suggestion that

he go to the patio and wait for her? Have you had a similar experience?

2. Describe the author's contrasting response when awakened by his wife on Sunday morning? Can you relate a similar experience?

3. What was the state of their relationship after church? How did they correct the problem?

4. What is the double bind? Relate how these forces work against each other in your marriage.

5. List the order of priorities suggested in chapter 10. Carefully consider if this order is true for you.

APPLICATION EXERCISE FOR MARRIAGE

Take the suggestion from chapter 10 and establish one night a week for dinner alone with your spouse. Alternate between going to a restaurant and dining at home. If your children are small, make it a late evening candlelight dinner after they are in bed. If you are morning persons, try a weekly breakfast *alone*. Feed your children first, then go out to a restaurant.

SESSION 7

Review chapters 11 and 12.

CONTENT SUMMARY

These two chapters point out the vulnerability of extramarital relationships and the ease by which one can fall into that trap. Everyone deserves and needs the feelings that are deceptively experienced in a developing affair. But these needs and feelings can come from your spouse within the marriage. The steps for restoration of trust using biblical principles of confession and forgiveness are also presented.

GOAL

To help you avoid an extramarital relationship through a fuller understanding of the pitfalls. If infidelity has occurred in your marriage, this section will help you find the road to restoration.

QUESTIONS FOR DISCUSSION

1. What were some of the early signs of problems for the man in chapter 11 who had an affair?

2. Discuss some of the risks of becoming overly extended in doing for others at your own expense.

3. Describe the feelings that this man experienced while driving his secretary home after working late. Explore ways that you and your spouse can create those same feelings together as a couple.

4. Why is confession so difficult when vows have been broken? Can you identify similar feelings when faced with making a confession to your spouse?

5. What is the true basis for forgiveness as related by Judy in chapter 12?

APPLICATION EXERCISE FOR MARRIAGE

1. If you or your spouse has broken your marriage vows and not yet dealt with this infidelity in your marriage, I ask you to prayerfully consider going through the steps of confession and forgiveness as outlined in chapter 12. If you do, I encourage you to consult a qualified third person, such as your pastor, church elder, deacon, or professional counselor, to guide you and pray for you during this process.

2. Take steps to create an experience with your spouse that gives you the ingredients of the excitement that lures people into affairs. Seek a special activity at least once a month that is devoted exclusively to having fun with your spouse. Here are some suggestions:

- Picnic in the country
- Plan a weekend at a hotel
- Spend an afternoon away from home with no plans—total spontaneity
- Attend an auction
- Go biking, hiking, boating, skiing, fishing, to concerts, art galleries, etc.
- Check out different restaurants

SESSION 8

Review chapter 13.

CONTENT SUMMARY

This chapter focuses on the power of submission in bonding a marriage. Frequently couples fall into power struggles. The problem comes when submission is viewed as a form of weakness. This chapter clearly shows the strength of submission and the work it does in our marriage.

GOAL

To show couples how mutual submission in marriage is a key to unity, service, and true authority.

QUESTIONS FOR DISCUSSION

1. What permanently removed the power struggle between George and Claire in chapter 13? Have similar situations occurred in your marriage?
2. Why is it inaccurate to assume that the counterpart of submission in marriage is dominance?
3. What is the source of true authority?
4. Recall an incident when submission seemed to bring about a positive response by your spouse.
5. According to the Greek translation *kephale,* what does the word *head* mean in Ephesians 5:23? Compare this definition to the traditional understanding of the word *head* in that passage of Scripture.

APPLICATION EXERCISE FOR MARRIAGE

1. Select a chore your spouse routinely does and do it for one week. Have your spouse share his or her feelings after you have performed that task. Now reverse the process and allow your spouse to do the same for you. Share your response. Is your motivation to serve each other heightened by this exercise?
2. List several selected tasks that require shared effort. Examine how unity and mutual service makes each of you stronger in the performance of your individual function.

SESSION 9

Review chapter 14.

CONTENT SUMMARY

This chapter shows that the element of fun is necessary to fully experience and enjoy intimacy in your marriage. Fun is not primarily an activity but rather a feeling that one experiences while doing a given activity. Therefore, as you search for fun experiences, you are directed to measure the anticipated feeling you will have instead of the fun of the activity itself.

GOAL

To show that fun in marriage is spontaneous, shared, and necessary. Fun can also create a safe environment to discuss more serious subjects.

QUESTIONS FOR DISCUSSION

1. How did the wife of the motorcyle rider solve her problem? Can you relate a time when you used a similar tactic in your marriage?
2. What was the key to Tim and Sally's successful "Pamper in Pink" weekend at the hotel?
3. How did fun create a safe setting for Carla's confession to Jack? Can you relate a time when you were having fun with your spouse and the experience opened the door for a serious discussion?
4. List the four essentials for a couple to experience fun. How do these work in your marriage?
5. Contrast the role of fun and discipline with each other. Share a time in your marriage when fun was present after a disciplined effort.

APPLICATION EXERCISE FOR MARRIAGE

1. Do something together spontaneously and examine how you feel about it after you have finished.
2. Do a disciplined task together and then reward yourself with a shared fun activity. Discuss later the part that the task played in making the activity a success.

SESSION 10

Review chapters 15, 16, and 17.

CONTENT SUMMARY

The concluding three chapters remind us that the care for the marriage goes beyond the couple alone. The extended family and the church need to support and nurture newlyweds as well as other couples. People caring for people is essential in the maintaining of good marriages as well as in the healing of hurting ones.

GOAL

To realize the positive role your church and extended family can play in the security of marriage.

QUESTIONS FOR DISCUSSION

1. Read 1 Corinthians 12:25–27 and discuss how this relates to the church's role and authority in caring for marriages.
2. Recall those first weeks of marriage after your wedding. Did you have the support of your family and church community? How did the support or the lack of that support affect you?
3. Review the following seven keys to determine if you have the plus element in your marriage.

   a. *Relationship*—Do you put the needs of your marriage ahead of your personal desires?
   b. *Giving*—Do you focus on what you can give to your spouse instead of what you can get?
   c. *Adjustment*—Are you able to see your marriage as a dynamic process in which you are able to make changes in your attitude and behavior for the happiness and well-being of your spouse?
   d. *Communication*—Are you communicating regularly with your spouse, creating the closeness that feeds your marriage?
   e. *Spontaneity*—Is there time in your marriage for impulsiveness? Can you think of a time recently when you and your spouse impulsively did something together that was fun?
   f. *Time*—Do you take time to provide experiences that are necessary in building your marriage and family relationship? Are traditions part of these experiences?
   g. *Christ-centeredness*—Is Jesus Christ the center of your marriage? Have you together invited Him to be Lord of your marriage? Do you daily read the Scriptures and pray together to maintain His position of lordship?

APPLICATION EXERCISE FOR MARRIAGE

1. Determine together specific changes you intend to make to create and maintain a strong, successful marriage. As a couple, write these changes in a letter to yourselves. Seal it, address it, and give it to a friend with the instruction to mail it to you in six

months. You may wish to continue this mechanism of accountability to help you care for your marriage.

2. Meet with other couples in your church and discuss ways in which you can support each other in your marriages. Here are some suggestions:

- Arrange couples' retreats at least one weekend a year. Leave children with babysitters.
- Have a Sweetheart's Banquet every Valentine's Day. Invite your pastor to lead you in the renewal of your marriage vows.
- As a group of couples, meet regularly for Bible study. Include in your meeting a time of sharing personal needs and a time to pray for one another. This group should also regularly plan a social activity.
- Always be sensitive to the Lord's leading to reach out to couples who need support and encouragement. Realize that a quality marriage does not happen automatically. It is the product of a lifetime of committed effort and mutual love.

Notes

CHAPTER 1

1. William H. Leach, *The Cokesbury Marriage Manual* (Nashville: Cokesbury Press, 1933), 31.

CHAPTER 2

1. Elisabeth Kübler-Ross, *On Death and Dying* (New York: Macmillan Co., 1969).
2. Malachi 2:16, RSV.

CHAPTER 3

1. Thomas A Harris, M.D., *I'm OK—You're OK* (New York: Harper & Row, 1967), 7.
2. Leach, *The Cokesbury Marriage Manual,* 25–30.
3. *Ibid.*
4. 2 Timothy 2:22.
5. Genesis 39:11, 12.
6. Leach.
7. James 4:13, 14.
8. 1 Corinthians 6:19, 20.
9. Genesis 2:24.

CHAPTER 4

1. "Loneliness Can Kill You," *Time,* Sept 5, 1977.
2. William Glasser, *Reality Therapy* (New York: Harper & Row, 1965), 9.
3. Acts 20:35.
4. Hosea 6:6.
5. 1 John 4:7.
6. Judson T. and Mary G. Landis, *Building a Successful Marriage,* Seventh Edition (New Jersey: Prentice-Hall, Inc., 1977), 63.

7. *Ibid.*, 381.
8. Don Beiswenger, M.A., consulting advisor for the Dependency Indicator.

CHAPTER 5

1. Hebrews 10:14.
2. John Powell, S. J., *Why Am I Afraid to Tell You Who I Am?* (Niles: Argus Communications, 1969), 20.
3. Romans 3:21, 22.

CHAPTER 7

1. Genesis 2:25.
2. "Biblical Perspectives on Marriage and Divorce," *The Standard,* Feb. 23, 1970.
3. Ephesians 5:32.
4. Genesis 2:25.

CHAPTER 9

1. Psalm 8:3, 9.

CHAPTER 10

1. Ecclesiastes 5:10–12.
2. *Time,* July 24, 1978.
3. *Minneapolis Star,* June 13, 1978.

CHAPTER 11

1. Hebrews 13:4.
2. 1 Corinthians 13:13.

CHAPTER 12

1. John 1:4, 5.
2. Oswald Chambers, *My Utmost for His Highest* (New York: Dodd, Mead, 1959), 12.
3. Psalm 37:23–25.
4. 1 Samuel 12:7.
5. 1 John 1:9.
6. Peter E. Gillquist, *Love Is Now* (Grand Rapids: Zondervan, 1970), 64.
7. James 5:16.
8. 1 Samuel 15:24–26.
9. 2 Samuel 12:13.
10. Psalm 51:4.
11. Psalm 51:16, 17.
12. Chambers, 61.
13. Exodus 9:34.

14. 1 Samuel 15:24, 25.
15. Matthew 6:14, 15.
16. Colossians 3:13.
17. V. Raymond Edman, *They Found the Secret* (Grand Rapids: Zondervan, 1960), 17.

CHAPTER 13

1. Luke 22:27.
2. Mickelsen, Berkeley, and Alvera, "Biblical Teaching about Men-Women Relationships."
3. Philippians 2:9–11.
4. Ephesians 5:1, RSV.
5. Acts 16:25.
6. John Powell, S. J., *Unconditional Love* (Texas Argus Communications, 1976), 65.
7. Genesis 2:24.
8. "The Head of the Epistles," *Christianity Today*, Feb. 20, 1981.
9. *Ibid.*
10. *Ibid.*
11. *Ibid.*
12. Genesis 2:21, 22.
13. Ephesians 5:31.

CHAPTER 15

1. 1 Corinthians 12:25–27.
2. Leontine Young, *The Fractured Family* (New York: McGraw-Hill, 1974), 140.

CHAPTER 16

1. Ephesians 5:21–33.